Street by Street

C000144591

COVEN...
RUGBY
BEDWORTH, BIRMINGHAM NEC, KENILWORTH

Baginton, Balsall Common, Dunchurch, Hampton in Arden, Hillmorton, Long Lawford, Meriden, Pickford, Tile Hill, Wolston

Ist edition May 2001

© Automobile Association Developments Limited 2001

This product includes map data licensed from Ordnance Survey® with the permission of the Controller of Her Majesty's Stationery Office. © Crown copyright 2000. All rights reserved. Licence No: 399221.

Published by AA Publishing (a trading name of Automobile Association Developments Limited, whose registered office is Norfolk House, Priestley Road, Basingstoke, Hampshire, RG24 9NY. Registered number 1878835).

Mapping produced by the Cartographic Department of The Automobile Association.

A CIP Catalogue record for this book is available from the British Library.

Printed by GRAFIASA S.A., Porto, Portugal

The contents of this atlas are believed to be correct at the time of the latest revision. However, the publishers cannot be held responsible for loss occasioned to any person acting or refraining from action as a result of any material in this atlas, nor for any errors, omissions or changes in such material. The publishers would welcome information to correct any errors or omissions and to keep this atlas up to date. Please write to Publishing, The Automobile Association, Fanum House, Basing View, Basingstoke, Hampshire, RG21 4EA.

Ref: ML034

Key to map pages	ii-iii
Key to map symbols	iv-1
Enlarged scale pages	2-3
Street by Street	4-75
Index – towns & villages	76
Index – streets	77-89
Index – featured places	89-91

ii

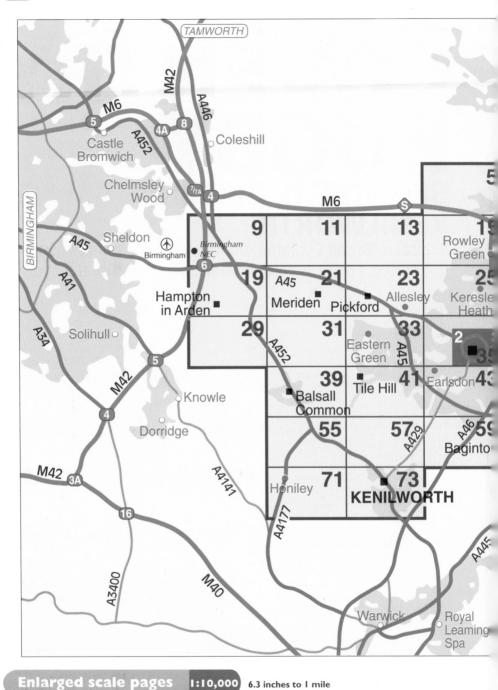

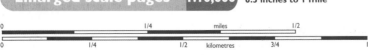

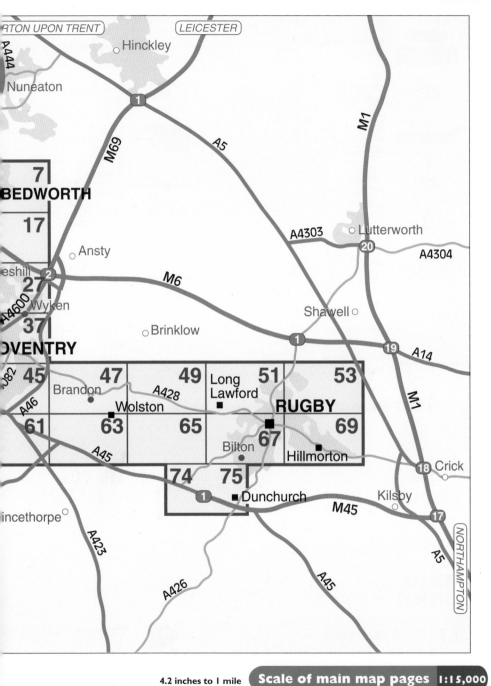

RTON UPON TRENT

LEICESTER

Hinckley

A444

Nuneaton

M1

M69

A5

7

BEDWORTH

17

Ansty

A4303

Lutterworth

20

A4304

eshill

2

M6

A4600

Wyken

Shawell

37

1

A14

OVENTRY

Brinklow

19

M1

082

45

47

A428

49

Long
Lawford

51

53

Brandon

A46

Wolston

RUGBY

61

63

65

67

69

A45

Bilton

Hillmorton

18 Crick

74

75

incethorpe

1

Dunchurch

Kilsby

17

A423

M45

A5

A426

A45

NORTHAMPTON

4.2 inches to 1 mile   **Scale of main map pages** **1:15,000**

| 0 | 1/4 | miles | 1/2 | 3/4 | 1 |
| 0 | 1/4 | 1/2 | kilometres 3/4 | 1 | 1 1/4 | 1 1/2 |

Junction 9	Motorway & junction	**P+**🚌	Park & Ride
Services	Motorway service area	🚌	Bus/Coach station
	Primary road single/dual carriageway	⇄	Railway & main railway station
Services	Primary road service area	■⇄	Railway & minor railway station
	A road single/dual carriageway	⊖	Underground station
	B road single/dual carriageway	⊖	Light Railway & station
	Other road single/dual carriageway	┼┼┼┼┼┼┼	Preserved private railway
	Restricted road	_LC_	Level crossing
	Private road	●—●—●—●	Tramway
← ←	One way street	- - - - - -	Ferry route
	Pedestrian street	··············	Airport runway
- - - - -	Track/ footpath	— · — · — · —	Boundaries- borough/ district
■■■■■■ ■■■■■■	Road under construction	▼▼▼▼▼▼▼	Mounds
[- - - -]	Road tunnel	**93**	Page continuation 1:15,000
P	Parking	**7**	Page continuation to enlarged scale 1:10,000

	River/canal, lake, pier	♿	Toilet with disabled facilities
	Aqueduct, lock, weir	⛽	Petrol station
465 ▲ Winter Hill	Peak (with height in metres)	PH	Public house
	Beach	PO	Post Office
	Coniferous woodland	📖	Public library
	Broadleaved woodland	𝒊	Tourist Information Centre
	Mixed woodland	♖	Castle
	Park	🏛	Historic house/ building
	Cemetery	Wakehurst Place NT	National Trust property
	Built-up area	Ⓜ	Museum/ art gallery
	Featured building	†	Church/chapel
⊓⊓⊓⊓⊓⊓⊓	City wall	⚑	Country park
A&E	Accident & Emergency hospital	🎭	Theatre/ performing arts
🚻	Toilet	🎥	Cinema

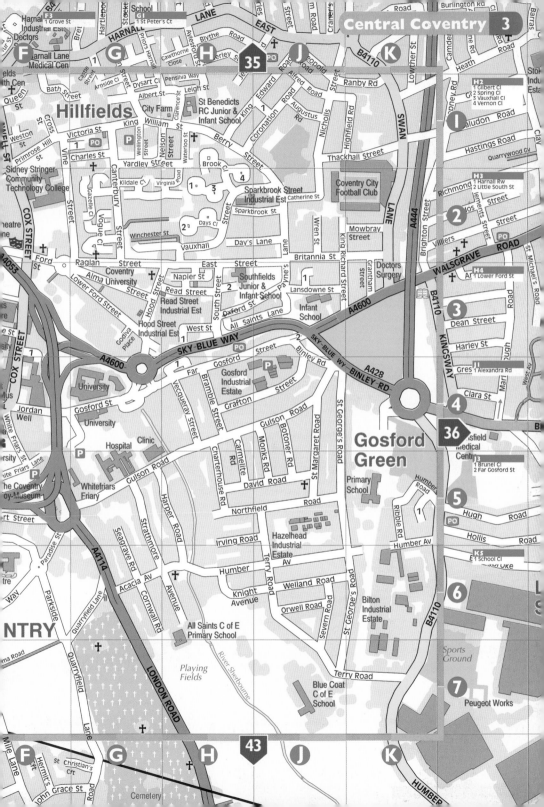

4

A   **B**   **C**   **D**

Cowley Wood

Green Lane

1

New Road

Sole End Farm

Astley La

Cov Lee

Coventry Way

Coventry Way

Breach Oak Farm

2

Taffs Farm

New Road

3

Breach Oak Lane

Smorrall Lane

Smorrall Lane

Highfield House Farm

4

Smorrall Lane

Corley Service Area

M6

5

Bennett's Road

A   North   **B**   **◀14**   Newland House Farm   **C**   **D**

Lane

Grove
Keresley

Lane

Newland Hall Farm

Newlan

pton

1 grid square represents 500 metres

E4
1 Hamilton Cl
2 Pembroke Cl
3 Ryhope Cl

F3
1 Himley Rd
2 Lindley Rd

E   F   G   H

F4
1 Pheasant Cl

F5
1 Newcomen Cl

G3
1 The Chestnuts
2 The Elms
3 The Firs
4 The Maples
5 The Rowans

G4
1 Topp's Heath

G5
1 The Tea Gdn

H4
1 All Saints Rd
2 Beechcroft
3 Walkers Wy

H3
1 Brooklea

Bedworth Lane

Woodlands Lane

Dove Cl

Bedworth Woodlands

Woodlands Road

Judd Cl

Charles Eaton Rd

Newtown Rd

Cozens Cl

Girtin Cl

Chalfont Cl

Suffolk

Ilford Cl

Deronda Cl

Sealand Dr

Mou
Plea

Newtown

Thomas St

John St

Gallagher Rd

Tarn Cl

Kirkston Rd

Ullswater Rd

Harrison Cres

The Views

The Willows

The Sycamores

The Laurels

Laburnum Cl

Heather Dr

Erica Av

Croft Rd

Croft Pool

Delame

Sharp

Smere Rd

3

6

Dalton Road

Astley Lane

Wilde Cr

Marriott Rd

The Lawns

Coventry Way

The Limes

Silver Birch Av

The Oaks

Coventry Way

Bedworth Rugby Football Club

Black

Rectory

Bentley Dr

Road

Whitburn Rd

Smercote Cl

Infant School

Anderton Road

Blair Dr

Keenan Dr

Dark Road

Keenan Dr

Smorrall Lane

Bellairs Av

Glebe Av

Martins Rd

Smith St

Renison Rd

Heath Road

Alice Close

Holyoak Cl

Hollyhurst

Howard Tyler Av

Jaffrey Cres

Butler Cres

Armson

Grant

Bedworth Heath

Goodyers End

Mayor

Newcomen Cres

Raynor Cres

Dowty Av

Howells Cl

Newey Av

Potters Rd

Kathleen Av

Henson Rd

Cashmore Rd

Hammersley St

Heath

Topp's Drive

Smarts Rd

Constance Cl

Hayes Gn

River Gn

Florence Cl

Marshall Rd

Field Cl

Robinson Rd

Melros Av

McMahon Rd

Lane

Maynard Av

Jeffrey Close

Humphrey Davy Rd

Moat Dr

Acorn

Farm

Goodyers End

Goodyers End County First School

Bowling Green Lane

St Giles School

Robert Road

Windmill Rd

Park Vw

David Rd

Heckley Rd

M6

Reach Brook

Royal Oak Lane

I5

High Ash Cl

Exhall Gn

Bruce Rd

Startin Cl

La

COVENTRY

PO

Bayto

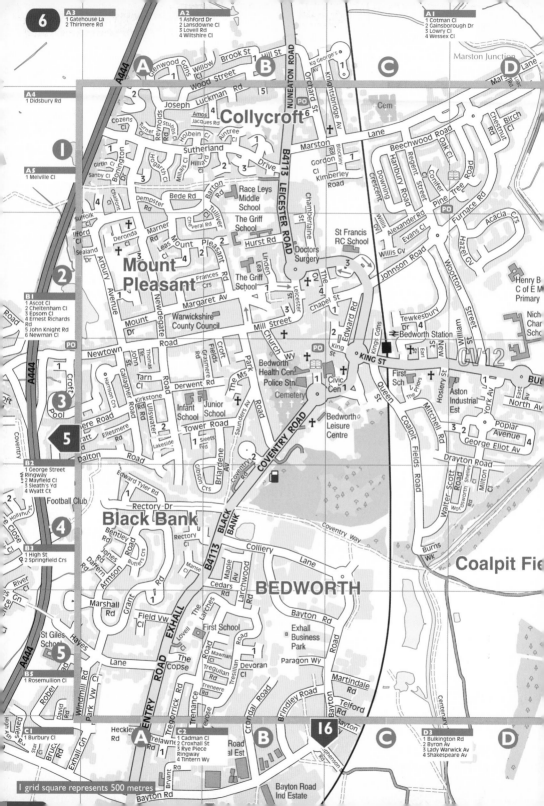

E F G H

G2
1 Thames Cl

H2
1 Brampton Wy
2 Carlton Cl

H3
1 Campling Cl

The Birches

ROAD

I

Claremont Close

Weston in Arden

Hotel

Weston

Lane

Farndon Cl

B4112

2

Mill Lane

The Paddocks

Kingsley Crs

Weston In Arden Junior & Infant School

2

1

Road

Cleveland

Severn Rd

Clyde Rd

1

Mersey Rd

Larkin

Barbridge

Glendon Gdns

Staples Rd

Ribble Cl

Road

Barbridge

Nun

Trent

Tamar

Calder Cl

Wye Cl

Weston Lane

Hemsworth Dr

Bulking C of E School

BEDWORTH   ROAD

Bedworth Rd

B4029

The Cft

3

SCHOOL RD

School Rd

B402

B4029

Weston Lawns Farm

Benn

Dingley Rd

1

Bedworth Road

Leyland

Villa Crs

Villa

1

Chequer St

Leicester St

2

PO

Staff

Neale

Barnacl

Bulkingt

4

B4109

ROAD

COVENTRY

5

ollyhurst

Coventry Wy

E F I7 G H

Top Road

LANE

8

A B C D

Solihull Parkway

STONEBRIDGE

Solihull Parkway

A452

ROAD

I

Lane

Lane

Blackfirs

B4438

ILL PARKWAY

A452

A446(T)

Litt
Pac

2

Fishpool Lane

Packington La

Bickenhill
Plantations

3

Northway

North
Av

Park Farm

xhibition Way

Perimeter

National
Exhibition Centre

Middle Bickenhill Lane

Industrial Est

PO

Underpass

Road

Pendigo Wy

B40

Perimeter Road

Harbet Dr

E Car Pk Rd

Pendigo Wy

4

i

Pendigo Wy

Perimeter
Rd

5

Pendigo

Wy

Perimeter
Rd

East Way

South Way

Middle
Bickenhill

S Car Pk Rd

East   Way

Coventry   Road

A Junction 6 B I8 ational
otorcycle
Museum C StonDrid

M4

Old Stat

Pasture

1 grid square represents 500 metres

E F G H

I

2

3

10

4

5

E F **19** G H

Broadwater

Hotel

Packington Park

Packington Hall

Hall Pool

Great Pool

The Mill Farm

River Blythe

BIRMINGHAM ROAD

RY ROAD

KENILWO

Packingto

The 'Deco

Geary's Heath

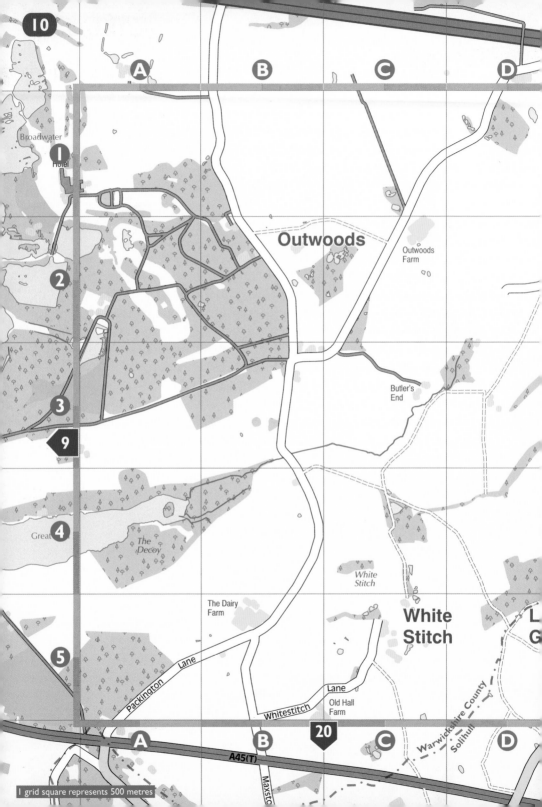

10

A B C D

Broadwater

1 Hotel

Outwoods

Outwoods
Farm

2

3

9

Butler's
End

4
Great

The
Decoy

White
Stitch

The Dairy
Farm

**White
Stitch**

L
G

5

Packington Lane

Whitestitch Lane

Old Hall
Farm

Warwickshire County

Solihull

A B **20** C D

A45(T)

Maxst

I grid square represents 500 metres

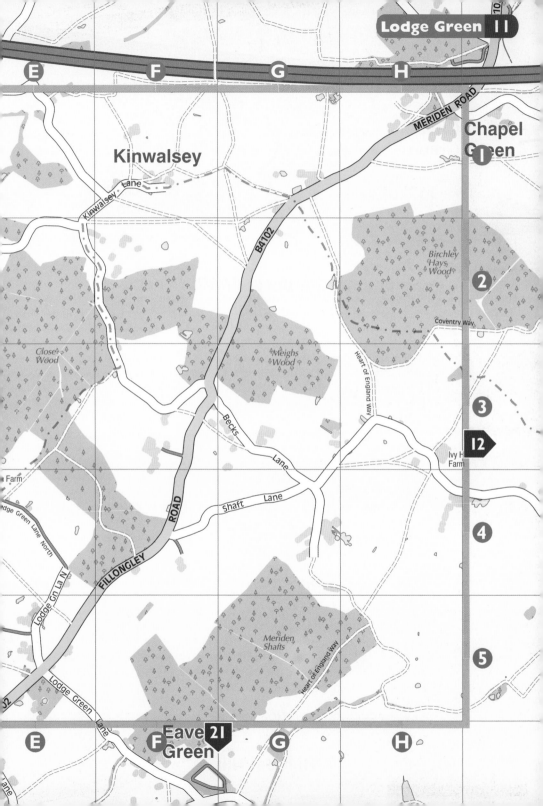

E F G H

Kinwalsey

MERIDEN ROAD

Chapel Green

Kinwalsey Lane

B4102

Birchley Hays Wood

2

Coventry Way

Close Wood

Meighs Wood

Heart of England Way

3

12

Becks Lane

Ivy H Farm

Farm

Shaft Lane

4

Lodge Green Lane North

FILLONGLEY ROAD

Lodge Gn La N

Meriden Shafts

Heart of England Way

5

E F G H

Lodge Green Lane

Eave Green 21

HollyHrst

E **F** **G** **H**

7

COVENTRY

Top

Road

I

MILE TREE LANE

Coventry Way

COVENTRY ROAD B4109

Spring Rd

Top Road

Park Farm

Chapel La

Barnacle

2

Lower Road

Sowe Fields Farm

Shilton Lane

3

Coventry Way

Warwickshire County

Coventry

4

Noonhill Farm

Shilton Lane

5

Centenary Way

Brookfield Farm

E **F** **27** **G** **H**

Woodway Lane

Sowe Common

Shilton Lane

Cem

Rowan Gv

mbleside

 mere

ane

Potters Green

brook

and

wood

HINC

E
F
9
G
H

BIRMINGHAM ROAD

VENTRY ROAD

I

Geary's Heath

KENILWORTH ROAD

Warwickshire County

Solihull

The Somers

2

Somers Road

ddington Lane

Molands Bridge

A452

HAMPTON LANE

Heath Farm

B4102

North Warwickshire Golf Club

3

20

River Blythe

MERIDEN ROAD

Patrick Bridge

Cornets End Lane

KENILWORTH ROAD

4

Hornbrook Farm

5

ton in Arden

Mercote Mill Farm

E
F
29
G
H

sh Lane

Park Farm

20

Pe...gton Lane

A

Whitestitch Lane

B

10

...d Hall ...rm

Warwickshire County

Solihull

Stitch
C2
1 Whichcote Av

C

Gre

D

A45(T)

BIRMINGHAM ROAD

Forest Hall

Maxstoke Lane

Maxstoke Close

Kittermaster Road

Archery Road

Meriden C of E School

Highfield

FILLONGLEY ROAD

B4102

Somers Road

I

2

Arden Cl

PO

Fairfield Ri

The Croft

Glovers Cl

Lodge

Alspath Road

Leymere Close

Levs Lane

Meriden

HAMPTON LANE

Strawberry Fields

Waterfall

1

MAIN ROAD

B4102

Hotel

North Warwickshire Golf Club

Heath Farm

Berkswell Road

Old School House Surgery

3

19

4

Cornets End

5

...cote Mill ...m

A

Park Farm

B

30

...oad

C

D

Back Lane

Ua...

Four Oaks

I grid square represents 500 metres

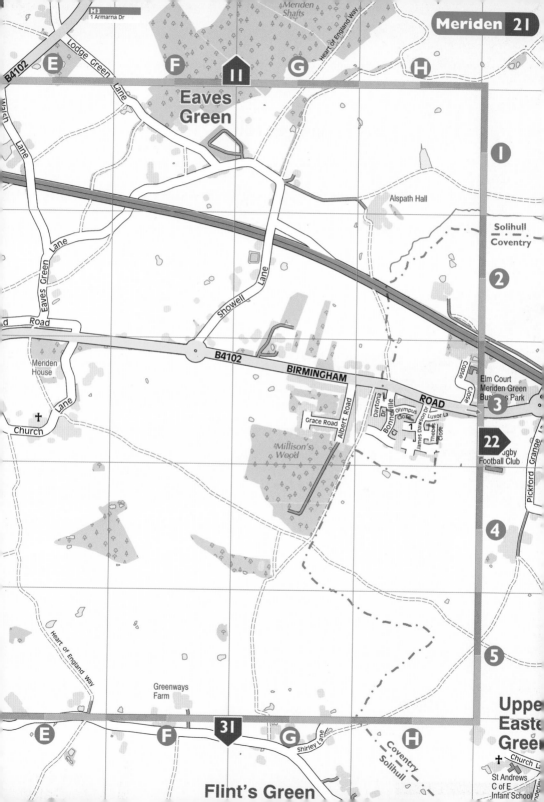

H3
1 Armarna Dr

Meriden Shafts

Eaves Green

Heart of England Way

Lodge Green Lane

B4102

March Lane

Eaves Green Lane

Snowell Lane

Road

Meriden House

Church Lane

Alspath Hall

Solihull
Coventry

B4102 **BIRMINGHAM**

ROAD

Grace Road

Albert Road

Daytona Dr

Bonneville Cl

James Dawson Dr

Olympus Close

Thebes Close

Luxor La

1

Copse Close

Elm Court
Meriden Green
Business Park

Rugby
Football Club

Pickford Grange

Millison's Wood

Heart of England Way

Greenways Farm

Shirley Lane

Coventry
Solihull

Uppe Easte Green

Church La

St Andrews
C of E
Infant School

Flint's Green

E F G H

1 2 3 4 5

I

22

31

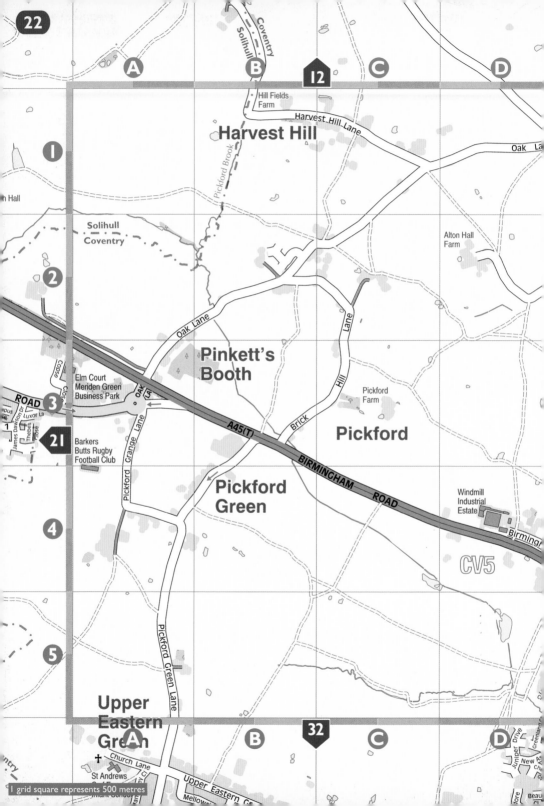

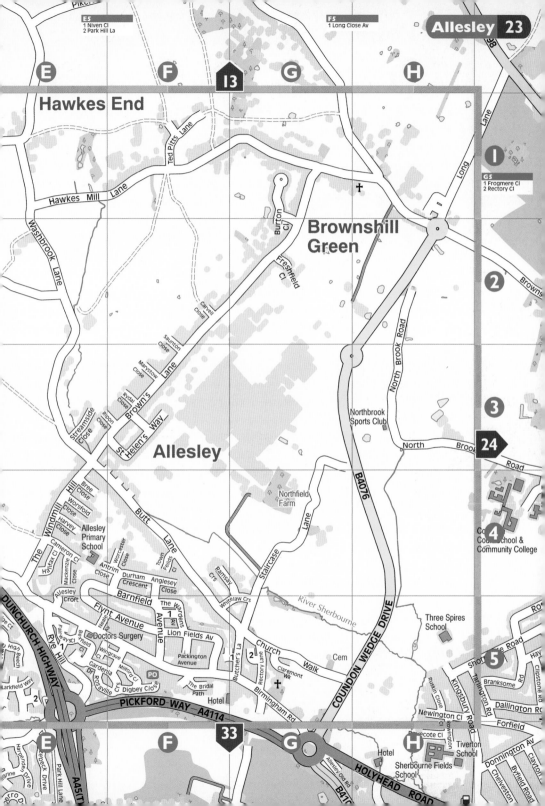

Hawkes End

Brownshill Green

Allesley

E 5
1 Niven Cl
2 Park Hill La

F 5
1 Long Close Av

G 5
1 Frogmere Cl
2 Rectory Cl

E F **13** G H

I

2

3

24

4

5

E F **33** G H

Hawkes Mill Lane

Washbrook Lane

Streamside Close

Ted Pitts Lane

Burton Cl

Freshfield Cl

Carvell Close

Saunton Close

Marystow Close

Lane

Brown's Way

Rydal Close

Ripon Close

St Helen's Way

Butt Lane

Long Lane

Browns

North Brook Road

Northbrook Sports Club

North Brook Road

B4076

Northfield Farm

Staircase Lane

Ramsay Crs

Whitelaw Crs

River Sherbourne

COUNDON WEDGE DRIVE

Three Spires School

Co...
Coun... School &
Community College

Shortle Road

Kingsbury Road

Tarlington Rd

Ro...

Hay...

Branksome Rd

Dallington Rd

Ruskin Close

Newington Cl

Forfield

Windmill Hill

Bree Close

Worsfold Close

Harvey Close

The

Cameron Close

Halifax Close

Mackenzie Close

Antrim Close

Allesley Croft

Worcester Close

Town Fields

Anglesey Close

Durham Crescent

Flynt Avenue

Barnfield

Avenue

The Wardens
1 Av

Lion Fields Av

Neale Av

Fair...Cl

Be...field

Rye Hill

DUNCHURCH HIGHWAY

Gardenia Dr

Wingrave Cl

Milford Cl

Rosville

Digbey Clo...

PO

The Bridal Path

Hotel

Packington Avenue

Doctors Surgery

Butcher's La

Rectory Lane

Church Walk

Claremont Wk

Cem

Birmingham Rd

PICKFORD WAY A4114

A45(T)

Larkfield Way

High...

...grine

Hazeleach...

...rro

Harpenden Drive

Zepeck Drive

Park Hill Lane

A45(T)

Allesley Primary School

Allesley Old Rd

HOLYHEAD ROAD

B4...

Sherbourne Fields School

Hotel

Dovecote Cl

Tiverton School

Donnington Av

Byfield Rd

Cheveston...

Clay...

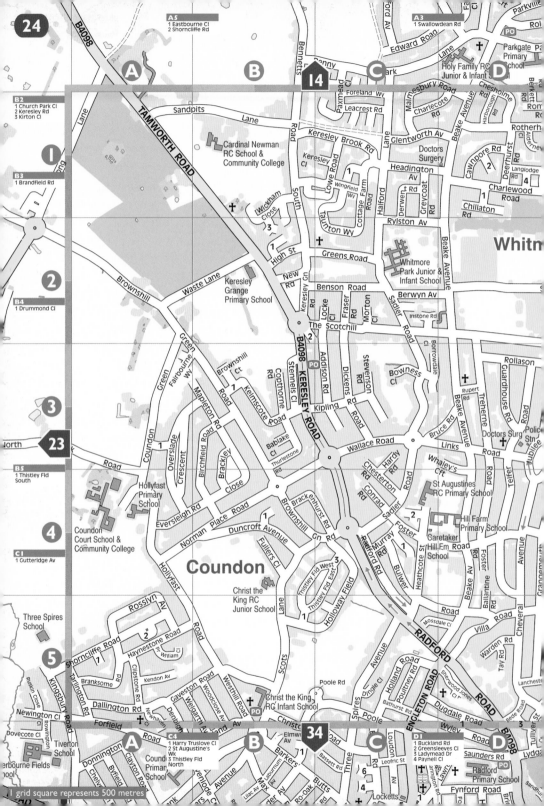

A5
1 Eastbourne Cl
2 Shorncliffe Rd

A3
1 Swallowdean Rd

B2
1 Church Park Cl
2 Keresley Rd
3 Kirton Cl

B3
1 Brandfield Rd

B4
1 Drummond Cl

B5
1 Thistley Fld
South

C1
1 Gutteridge Av

C4
1 Harry Truslove Cl
2 St Augustine's
Wk
3 Thistley Fld
North

D1
1 Buckland Rd
2 Greensleeves Cl
3 Ladymead Dr
4 Paynell Cl

A B 14 C D

I

2

3

23

4

5

Coundon

Whitm

1 grid square represents 500 metres

34

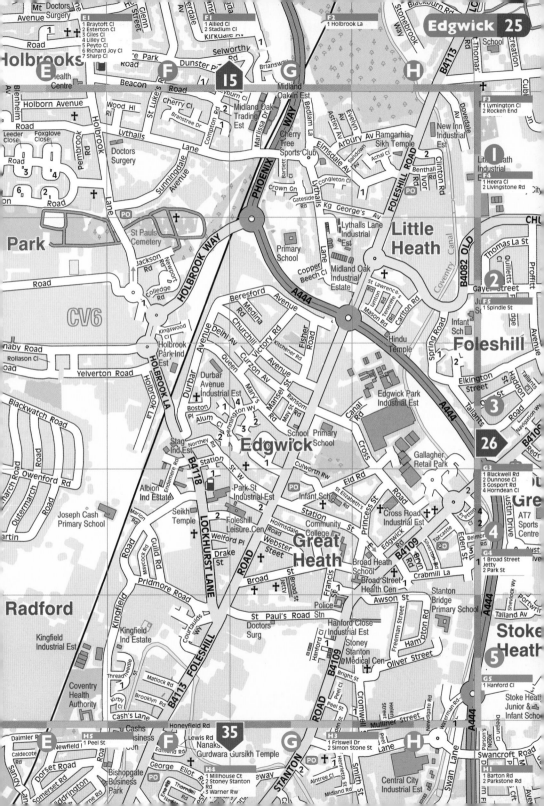

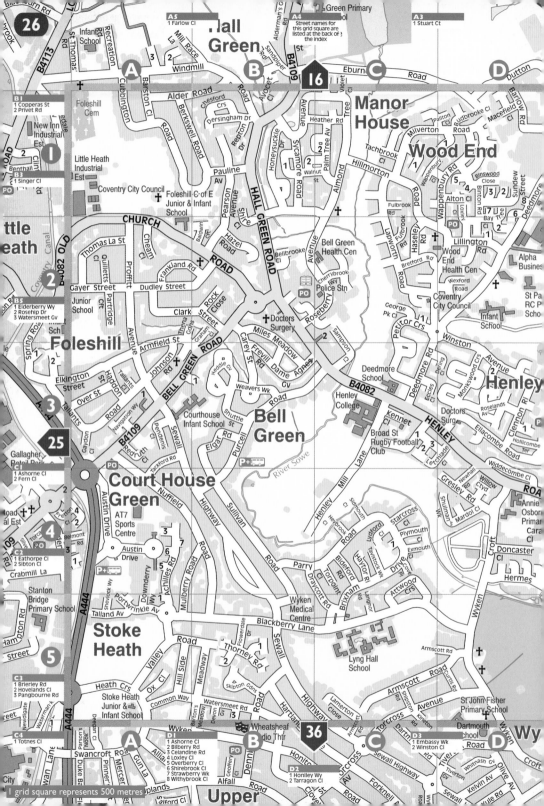

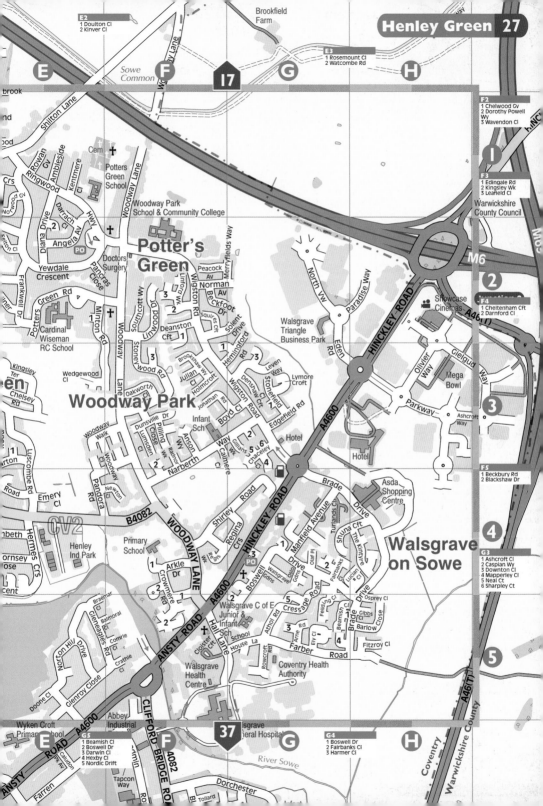

E2
1 Doulton Cl
2 Kinver Cl

Brookfield Farm

E3
1 Rosemount Cl
2 Watcombe Rd

E · F · 17 · G · H

Sowe Common

Woodway Lane

Shilton Lane

brook

F2
1 Chelwood Gv
2 Dorothy Powell Wy
3 Wavendon Cl

1

F3
1 Edingale Rd
2 Kingsley Wk
3 Leafield Cl

Warwickshire County Council

M6

Rowan Gv
Ambleside
Kentmere
Cem
Potters Green School
Ringwood
Darrach
Angela Av
PO
Hwy
Diana Drive
Barrach
Woodway Lane
Woodway Park School & Community College

Crs
Fenton Cl
Frankwell Dr
Yewdale Crescent
Pancras Close
Milton Rd
Doctors Surgery

Potter's Green

Merryfields Way
Peacock Av
Norman Av
Linford Wk
Wigston Rd
Beckfoot
squires Cft
Solent Drive
Deanston Cft

North Vw
Paradise Way

2
Junction 2

F4
1 Cheltenham Cft
2 Darnford Cl

Showcase Cinemas
A46(T)

Kingsley Ter
Chelsey Rd
en
Potters Green Rd
Cardinal Wiseman RC School
Wedgewood Cl

Woodway Park

Woodway Lane
Stoneywood Rd
Linhill
Oakworth
Brookshaw Wy
Julian
Holmcroft
Jonathan Rd
Hemingford
Leven Way
Stonefield
Denshaw Wy
Lymore Croft
Stonefield Cft
Edgefield Rd
Wigston Road
Boyd Rd

Eden Rd

Walsgrave Triangle Business Park

Olivier Way
Gielgud Way
Mega Bowl
Parkway
Ashcroft Way

3

Woodway Walk
Dunsville Dr
Pilling Close
Lumsden
Anson Rd
Radmor
Narberth
Infant Sch
Way
Gillians
Calmere
Chaceley
Hotel

Hotel

Asda Shopping Centre

F5
1 Beckbury Rd
2 Blackshaw Dr

Luscombe Rd
Emery Cl
Pandora Rd
New Eaton
Woodway Walk
Hermes Crs
CV2
Henley Ind Park
B4082
WOODWAY LANE
Primary School
Shirley Road
Regina Crs
HINCKLEY ROAD
Brade Drive
Turlands Cl
Shuna Cft
The Kintyre
Walsgrave on Sowe

4

G3
1 Ashcroft Cl
2 Caspian Wy
3 Downton Cl
4 Mapperley Cl
5 Neal Ct
6 Sharpley Ct

beth
ornsey
ose
cent

Braemar
Gleneagles Rd
Balmoral
Comrie
Crathie
Arkle Dr
Crowmere
Boswell Rd
Walsgrave Gdns
PO
Manfield Avenue
Oslo
Olaf Pl
Cross
Fairbanks
Osprey Rd
Lulan
Beamish
Gibbs
Barlow
Fitzroy Cl

Norton Hill Drive
Doone Cl
Glenroy Close
ANSTY ROAD
A4600
Hall Lane
Cloister Cft
House La
Rowcroft Rd
Walsgrave C of E Junior & Infant School
Arne Rd
Athol Rd
Ely Cl
Feilding Cl
Farber Road
Brade Drive

5

Abbey Industrial
Wyken Croft Primar
CLIFFORD BRIDGE RO
A4082
Walsgrave General Hospital
Coventry Health Authority
Walsgrave Health Centre

G5
1 Beamish Cl
2 Boswell Dr
3 Darwin Cl
4 Hexby Cl
5 Nordic Drift

G4
1 Boswell Dr
2 Fairbanks Cl
3 Harmer Cl

E · F · 37 · G · H

ANSTY ROAD A4600
Farren
Caludon
Pk Av
Tapcon Way
Dorchester Way
Bl
Tollard

River Sowe

Coventry
Warwickshire County
A46(T)

28

SOLIHULL ROAD B4102

M42

A **B** **18** **C** **D**

Hampton Manor Homes

PO

Infant School

Elm Tree

Peel Close

The Surgery

Belle Vue

Bellem Road

Hook End

1

2

Lane

Eastcote Lane

Eastcote Lane

Eastcote Lane

3

Barston Lane

Walsal End Lane

Walsal End

Wharley Hall

Eastcote

4

Knowle Road

Wood Lane

Barston Lane

Oak Lane Farm

Oak Lane

5

River Blythe

Wood Lane

Brook Green Lane

A **B** **C** Hob Lane **D**

Bar

Barsto

1 grid square represents 500 metres

E F 19 G H

I Park Fa

Mer Mill
Far

Arden
House

Marsh Lane

River Blythe

A452

2

Ryton
End

**Bradnock's
Marsh**

KENILWORTH

3

ROAD

30

Marsh Lane

Bradnocks Lane

4

Wootton Lane

Wootton Green

Blythe House

5

Heart of England Way

Wootton

E F G H

Barston

E

F

21

G

H

Heart of England Way

Greenways Farm

Shirley Lane

Coventry Solihull

Upper East Green

✝ Church

St Andrews of E. Infant School

I

Orchard Dr

Morg Rd

Flint's Green

Hockley

2

Coventry Way

Hill House Farm

Broad Lane

Coventry Solihull

3

The Moat

32

Benton Green

Benton Green Lane

Rough Close

4

ower arm

Victoria Farm

Patrcia Close

5

Mae

TANNERS' LANE

E

Moat House Farm

F

Coventry Way

39

Spencer's Lane

G

H

Coventry Solihull

Reeves Green

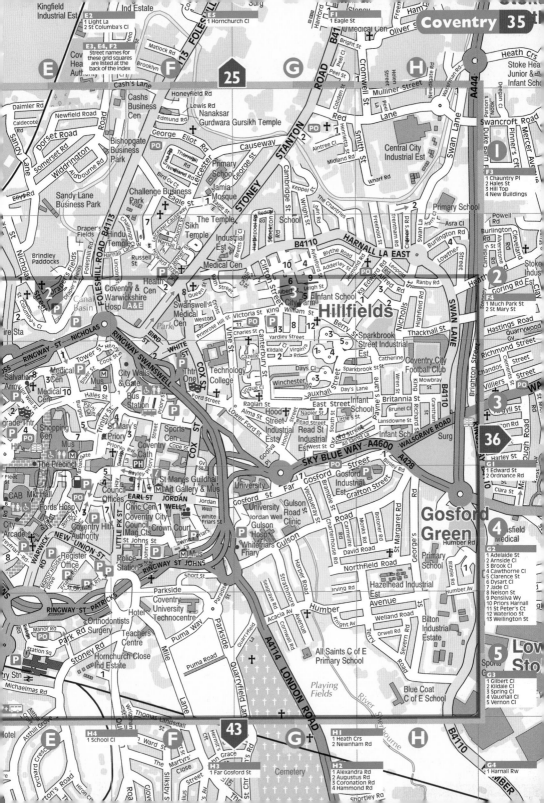

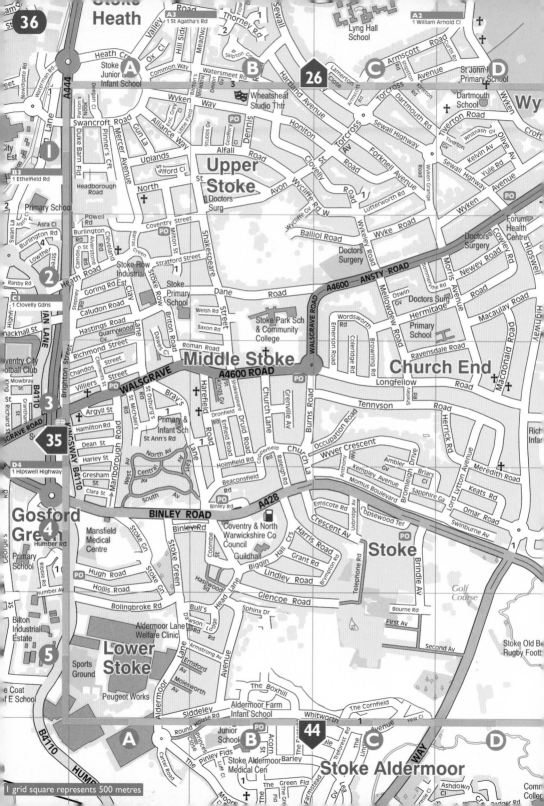

E5
1 Arthingworth Cl
2 Windermere Av

F1
1 Snape Rd

Norton Hill
Glenroy Close
Comrie

Cloister Cft
House La
Farber
Ely
Roy Cl

Walsgrave
Health Centre

Coventry Health
Authority

Rowcroft

E   **F**   **27**   **G**   **H**

Wyken Croft
Primary School

ANSTY ROAD A4600

Abbey
Industrial
Estate

Walsgrave
General Hospital

River Sowe

Coventry

Warwickshire County

A46(T)

I

F2
1 Frampton Wk
2 Westmorland Rd

Caludon Pk Av
Farren
Road
Bodmin
Road
Tapcon Way

B4082

Dorchester

Abbey
Industrial Est

Infant
School

Arch Road
Edyth Rd
Belgrave
Road
Westmorland Road
Emmerdale
Dalton Gdns
Keswick Wk
Blandford
Drive
Tollard
Cranborne
Corfe Cl
Cha

Tarran
Wareham Gn
Way

Bridport Close

2

F4
1 Melfort Cl
2 Rannock Cl

St Austell Road
Attoxhall
Sandilands Cl
Akhnome
CLIFFORD BRIDGE ROAD B4082
Marnhull
Wk
La
Wimborne
Dr
Wimborne Drive
Studland
Warmwell
Cl

Abbotsbury Cl

Fontmell Cl

Porchester
Way
Sturminster Cl

Coombe
Pool

3

The
Woodlands

Doctors'
Surgery
Coventry City
Council
Triumph
Cl
Ventnor Cl
Harry
Rose
Road
School

Glebefarm
Gv

Bridgeacre
Gardens

Faygate
Royston Cl

Gainford Rise

Fieldside
Abbeydale
CLIFFORD BRIDGE ROAD
Coombe Pk Road

Primary School

G2
1 Bryanston Cl
2 Shillingstone Cl
3 Swanage Gn

Lloyd Crs
Standish Cl
Crakston Cl
Allerton Cl
Billinton
Brewster Cl
Drive
Barbican Ri
Rigdale
Dunrose Cl
Margeson Cl

Bridgeacre
Gdns

Portree Av

Bracadle Cl

Dunvegan Cl

Brinklow
Rd

B4027

Coombe Ct

B402

4

G4
1 The Greensward
2 Grimston Cl
3 St Bart's Cl

Carver Cl

Colebrook Cl
Mill La

Coombe Pk Rd

Porchester
BRINKLOW ROAD
Harvesters

Hunters

Kelway
Kelway
Skipworth Road
Carnville
Mikey
Close

PO

BINLEY ROAD A428

Conifer Paddock
Ebro Crs
Ullswater Rd
Hothorpe Cl
Wilson Gn
Alvin
B4082
BRANDON ROAD

Harry Weston Rd
Orchard Ct
Braddock
Kerris Wy
Cheiney
Hargrave
Hepworth Road
Hulme
Lyttleton Cl
Dowley Cft
Newstead

Geo wale Av
Oweswater Rd
George Marston Rd
Princethorpe Way
Bowden Way
Foxton Road
Foxton
Newbold Cl
Wilson
Winch

Primary School
Haselbech

Ibex Cl
Cypress

Binley
Business
Park

Brewers

Sheldrake
Close

Homeward
Way

Broad Street
Old Boys Rugby
Football Club

5

ttesbrook
LawFord
Cults Cl
Way
Bruntingthorpe Wy
Willoughby Cl
Oxenden
Grange
Gayhurst

Tysoe
Santos
Granborough Cl
Flamboro
Flamborough Cl
Stirling Cl
Falcon
Kestrel
Rutland
Whissle
Whiteside Cl

Lane

Skipworth
Rd

A428

Brandon

E   **H5**
1 Brunton Cl
2 Bulwick Cl
   F   **45**   **G**   **H**

G5
1 Gaulby Wk
2 Hardwyn Cl
3 Soredale Cft
4 Tideswell Cl
5 Upperfield Wy

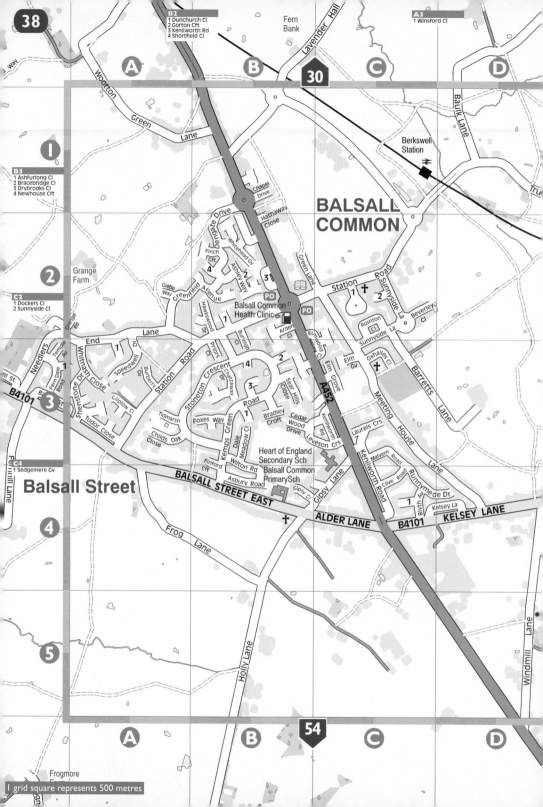

E F 31 G H TANNERS' LANE

Coventry Way

Moat House Farm

Spencer's Lane

Reeves Green

Coventry Solihull

I

Carol Green

Hodgett's Lane

B4101

NAILCOTE LANE

Duggins Lane

Lant Cl

Midla Cent the D

2

Nailcote Hall (Hotel)

Beechwood

B4101

3

40 ►

Cromwe

Waste Lane

WASTE LANE

Coventry Way

Hodgett's Lane

4

Catchems Corner

Hob Lane

Beanit Farm

5

Burton

Red Lane

e Firs

E F 55 G H Hob Lan

Burton Green Primary School

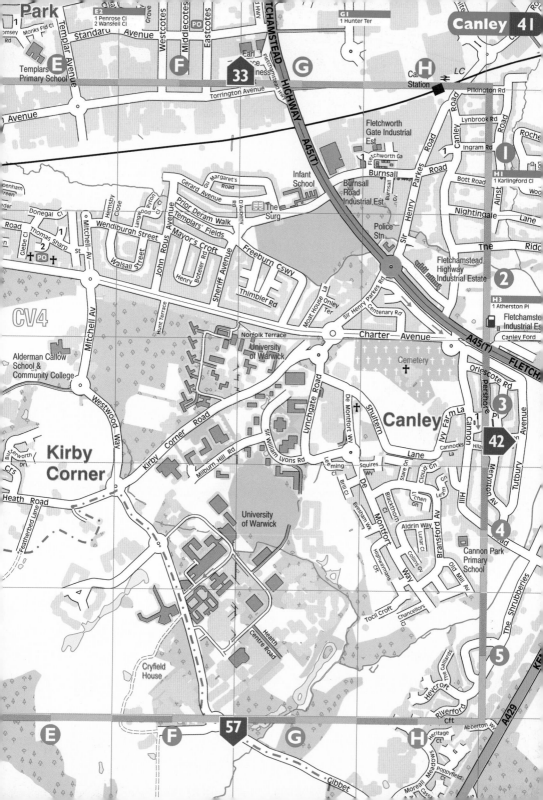

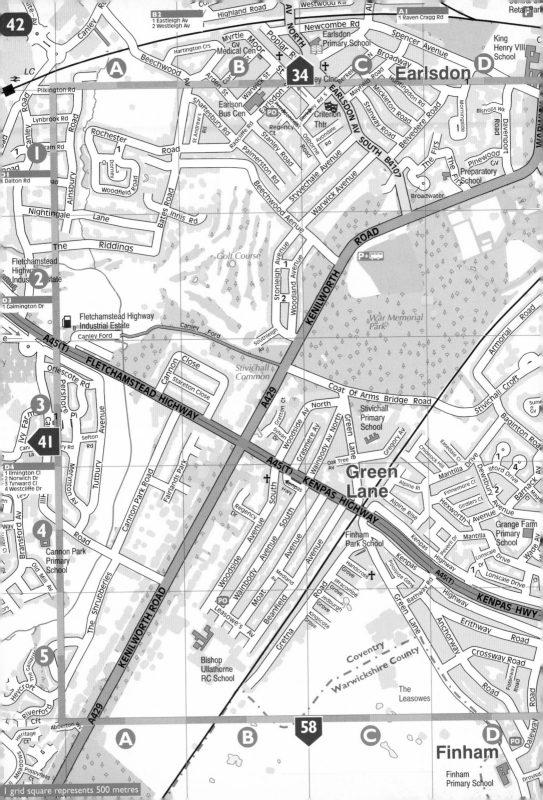

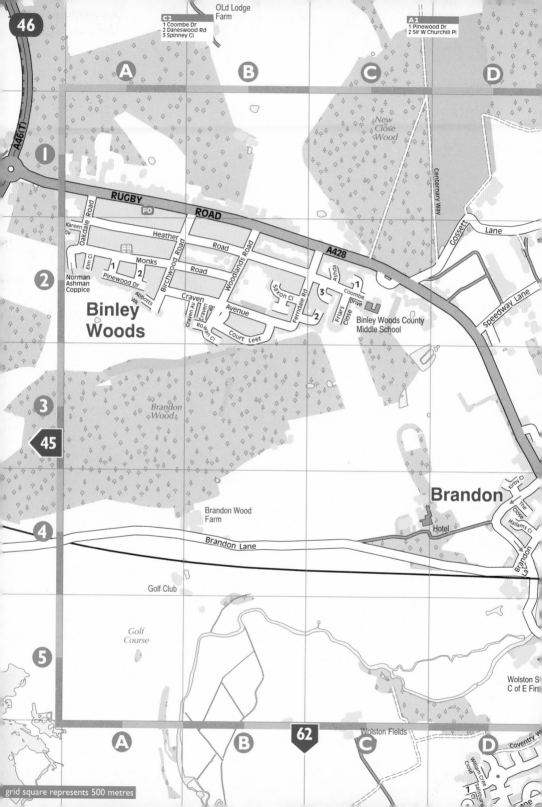

46

C2
1 Coombe Dr
2 Daneswood Rd
3 Spinney Cl

A2
1 Pinewood Dr
2 Sir W Churchill Pl

Old Lodge
Farm

A · B · C · D

I

New
Close
Wood

A46(T)

Centenary Way

RUGBY

PO

ROAD

A428

Gossett

Lane

Kareen
Gv

Oakdale Road

Heather

Road

2

Norman
Ashman
Coppice

Elm Cl

Pinewood Dr

Monks

1

2

Abbotts
Wk

Birchwood Road

Road

Woodlands Road

Craven

Craven Av

Craven
Gv

Avenue

Rowan Cl

Court Leet

Saxon Cl

Ferndale Rd

Asnda

Coombe
Drive

3

2

1

Friars
Close

Binley Woods County
Middle School

Speedway Lane

**Binley
Woods**

3

Brandon
Wood

45

Brandon

Kirby Cl

The
Close

Hallam's Cl

4

Brandon Wood
Farm

Brandon Lane

Hotel

Brandon La

5

Golf Club

Golf
Course

Wolston S
C of E Firs

A · **B** · **62** · **C** · **D**

Wolston Fields

Coventry W

William Cres
Close

Salisbury
Close

grid square represents 500 metres

ES
1 Willow Brook Rd

E

F

G

H

Brinklow
Heath

Hill Farm

I

QUEENS ROAD

2

Bretfor

Brandon Grange
Farm

BRANDON ROAD

A428

3

A

48

Garage

RUGBY ROAD

4

River Avon

B4455

Marston

5

Wolston
Business
Park

Hawthorne
Close

Priory Road

The
Priory

Meadow Road

Main Street

Police
Station

1

Elmdene
Close

Larchfields

Coalpit Lane

New Farm

Wolston
Surg

School Street

E

PO

Lammas Ct

Wolston

F

63

G

B4455

H

Warwick Road

Brook Street

1

Dyer's Lane

Cemetery

Coventry Way

B4455

A

B

C

D

Abbey Hall
Farm

QUEENS ROAD

1

Hill Farm

2

Bretford

Kings Newnham Lane

Newnham
Hall

River Avon

3

A428

47

Vicarage
Farm

Avon Ho

Dalton
Close

Kings Newnham

Fitzalan Close

COVENTRY

ROAD

Church
Lawford

Street

4

The
Grange

B4455

Hall

Lane

Coronation Road

5

arm

A

B

Lim
Hall

64

C

D

Limestone

E   F   G   H

Cathi.
Lane

Fennis Fields
Farm

Highfields

I

Little Lawford Lane

2

**King's
Newnham**

Little La

Clayhill Lane

3

50

Clayhill Farm

Clayhill Lane

4

St Jo
La

Church Road

✝

Cross

Judge
Close

Street

Long Lawford

West
St

Chapel
Street

Main
Street

Bailey
La

BY ROAD

Railway Street

A428

Livingstone Avenue

Green
Cl

The Green

5

South View Road

COVENTRY

ROAD

Mount
Pleasant

E   F   G   H

65

d Heath Lane

50

A Cathiron Lane
B **B4**
1 Edinburgh Wy
2 Okement Gv
3 Prentice Cl
4 Tamar Cl
5 Wavebeck Ct
6 Windrush Wy

Oxford Canal

Canal Walk

Cathiron Lane

C

D **A4**
1 Greenwood Cl

B4112

HARBOROUGH ROAD

Oxford Canal Walk

1

2 Lane

B5
1 Cherwell Wy
2 Lauderdale Cl

C4
1 Welland Cl

Little Lawford Lane

Little Lawford

MAIN STREE

Newbold Lei
Centre

Newbold
FC

Clayhill Lane

River Avon

3

Holbrook
Grange

Lea Crescent

49

D2
1 Manor House Cl

Home
Farm

Cemetery

St John's La

Thomas Way

Hirst Cl

3

Round Avenue **1**

Ashman Avenue

Holbrook Road

4

Tove Cl

4 Lane

The Spinney

Cross Street

1

Boyce Way

Garratt Close

2

Steeping Road

Thurnmill Road

ng Lawford

Judge Close

Street

Long Lawford
Combined School

Elizabeth Way

Arnet Dr

6

Weaver Dr

Chapel St

West St

Baileys

School Street

PO

Townsend

5

Cherwell Way

2

Railway Street

Main

5

tone Ave

w Road

The Green

Green

Back Lane

Lane

Briars Close

A428 RUGBY ROAD

66

A

B

C

D

Paynes

Somers Road

Upton

St Oswalds

1 grid square represents 500 metres

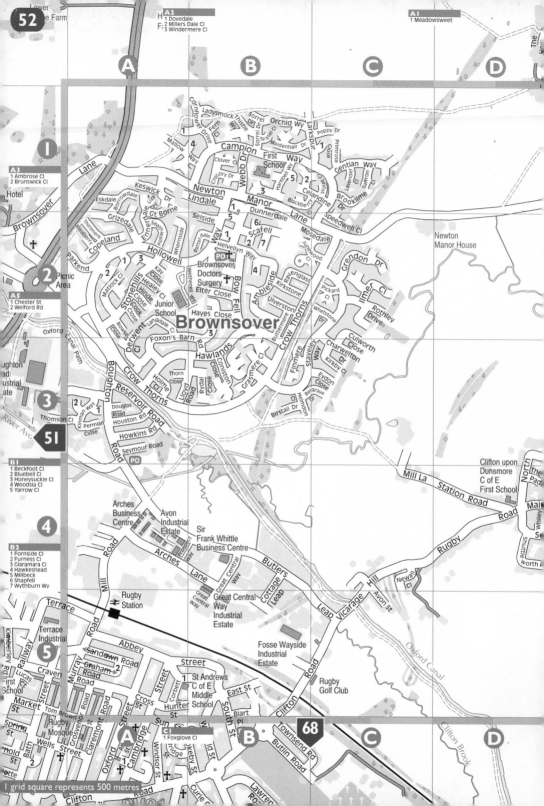

Main St

Little London Lane

Watling Crs

E   **F**   **G**   **H**

River Avon

1

Newton Road

Dunsmore Farm

2

Lane

Buckwell

Newton Road

3   R

emetery

Manor Farm

Buckwell Lane

Dunsmore

Church St

Robertson Cl

Hadfield Cl

Lilbourne Road

4

Orwell Cl

Everard Close

Clifton upon Dunsmore

Road

The Kent

Clifton Hall

5

E   **F**   **G**   **H**

69

Lane   Home Farm

Burton

E   F   **39**   G   H

Red Lane

Hob Lane

Burton Green
Primary School

1

e Firs

Black Hales
Farm

KENILWORTH ROAD

A452

2

Redfern
Manor

3

BIRMINGHAM ROAD

56

Chase Farm

4

Rudfyn
Manor

Little Chase
Farm

5

Warriors Lodge
Farm

Ea
Fa

Chase Lane   E   F   **71**   G   H

Pleasance Farm

56

Burton Green

Grange

Crackley Lane

40

Hurst Farm

A   **B**   **C**   **D**

Red Lane

Coventry Way

South Hurst
Farm

Burton Green
Primary School

1

2

Long Meadow
Barn Farm

3

55

Crackley
Wood

ROAD

Red Lane

Dunns Pitts
Farm

4

A452

Hollis Lane

5

Camp Farm

The
Spring

Chase Lane

East Chase
Farm

Priorsfield
Combined
School

A452   BEEHIVE HILL

St Augustines
R C Combined
School

Upper   Spring   Lane

B4103

FIELDGATE LANE

A   **B**   **C**   **D**

72

CLINTON LANE

Cobbs
Rd

Woodcote

Avenue

Priorsfield
Rd

De Montfort

Grange
Avenue

Quarry
Rd

Malthouse
Lane

Croft

Amherst Road

Fernhill
Close

Bromley

STREET

asance Farm

1 grid square represents 500 metres

G5
1 Butler Cl
2 Whitehead Dr

E

Cryfield
House

F

41

Health
Centre Road

G

H

Heycroft
Cft
Haverford
Cft

A429

KEN

Abberton Wy

Heritage
Ct

SMeadow

Poppyfield
Ct

I

Gibbet

Hill

Moreall
Meadows

Cassandra
Gr

The
Arboretum

Rd

The
Spinney

A429

Wainbody
Wood
School

2

Ltl
Cryfield

Cryfield Hts

Leighton Cl

Marshfield
Dr

Gibbe

Cryfield   Grange   Road

Cryfield
Grange

KENILWORTH   ROAD

A429

Beverly Dr

Stoneleigh   Road

3

58

4

Millburn
Grange

Centenary   Way

CV8

Princes Drive
Industrial Est

Princes Dr

Crackley

A429

Woodland   Rd

Leagh Cl

Common

Lane

5

Highland   Road

Inchbrook   Road

Finham   Brook

Crackley Lane

St Josephs
Convent School

COVENTRY   ROAD

Southfield Dr

Convent Cl

Littleton Close

Centenary Wy

Dalehouse Lane
Industrial
state

Best Av

7 1 2

Garlick Dr

ouse Lane

73

Fenny Way

Northvale

4 5
2

Lulworth   Cl

Clifden Gv

Frythe Cl

Centenary   Way

H

Lad es Hill

E

F

G

Hawkesworth

Alpine Ct

Lower Ladyes
Hills

Winc

Hills

Forge Rd

Mill End

BroomyDa

Greensward Cl

Knowle

Westonbirt

Fairw

A45(T) STONEBRIDGE HIGHWAY

Fenside Avenue

Leaf Lane

The Graylands

Alfriston Rd

Jacklin Drive

Rees Dr

Vardon Dr

Alfriston Road

Wychwood Av

Brentwood Av

Roman Wy

Roman Wy

Ivygrove

HOWES LANE

Mill Hill

A46(T)

Hadleigh Drive

Cotswold Dr

Carnford

St Martin's Rd

Oxley Dr

Leigh Av

Winsham Wk

Finham Gv

Howes Lane

Grange Av

B4115

St Martin's Rd

St Martin's Road

43

Hotel

Hill

Coventry Golf Course

Hall Drive

Holly Wk

Frances Rd

Coventry Road

Rowley Road

Lunt Roman Fort

PO

Kimberley Rd

Baginton

Church Road

Oak Close

River Stowe

60

B4113 ST MARTIN'S ROAD

COVENTRY ROAD

B4113

Stoneleigh Grange

Bubbenhall Bridge

E **Stoneleigh**

E   F   G   H

I

2

3

4

5

60

River Sowe

House King Henry
VIII School

STONEBRIDGE HIGHWAY

B4110

Park

London Rd

A45(T) A Stonebridge
Trading Est

Sibree Road

Rowley Dr

Rowley Drive

Stonebridge
Trading Est

B

44

Rowley Road

C

Coventry
Trading Est

Brandon La

D

Ryton
Bridge

LONE

Hotel

unt Roman
Fort

I

Rowley Road

Midland Air Museum

Woodhams
Road

Siskin Drive

Baginton

2

Oak Close

Coventry
Trading
Estate

Coventry
Airport

Siskin Parkway West

Coventry
Trading Estate

Siskin Parkway East

3

59

Siskin Parkway
East

Rock Farm

4

5

Bubbenhall
Bridge

River Avon

Centenary Way

A

B

C

PO

D

Bubbenhall

1 grid square represents 500 metres

G3
1 St Leonard's Wk

H2
1 Church Cl

E   F   **45**   G   H

Nature
Reserve

River Avon

1

A45(T)

Redland Lane

A45(T) — LONDON ROAD

Ryton-on-
Dunsmore

2

Chapel

Church Road

Centenary Way

Glenfern
Gdns

Field Vw

1

PO

3

62

Bagshaw Cl

Fetherston Crs

High Street

Crs

Handley's
Cl

1

Soden's Av

Centenary Way

OXFORD ROAD

Ryton
Lodge

Warren Field

Ryton-on-Dunsmore
C of E First School

LEAMINGTON ROAD

A445

Mann's Cl

4

Centenary Way

A423(T)

A445

5

E   F   G   H

OXFORD ROAD

Ryton
Pool

62

A B **46** C D

Course

D1
1 Millennium Wy

Wolston
C of E

Wolston Fields
Farm

Coventr

William Cree
Close
Salisbury
Close
Kelsey's Cl
Wolston Lane

1

2

Centenary Way

Grounds Farm

Centenary Way

Wolston Lane

Ryton Gardens

3

61

LONDON ROAD

ROAD

Grange Farm

4

5

Freeboard Lane

Plott Lane

Knightlow C of E
First & Middle
Schools

Squires Rd
Robert
Close

Moo
Farm
Close
Broo
Surg

ROAD

A Ryton
Heath m
B C D

School

Orchard
Way

1

1 grid square represents 500 metres

64

Ⓐ

Ⓑ

48

Ⓒ

Ⓓ

Limestone
Hall

Ⓘ

2

Rookery
Hall

3

Heath Farm

Lawford Lodge
Farm

63

4

Coalpit Lane

5

Manor
Farm

Wolston
Grange

Ⓐ

Ⓑ

Ⓒ

Ⓓ

Dunsmore
Heath

Home
Farm

I grid square represents 500 metres 5(T)

COVENTRY ROAD

View Road

Gree

E

F ount
Pleasant

49

G

H

I

Lawford Heath Lane

2

Lawford Heath Lane

Lawford Hill
Farm

3

66

4

Cawston
Farm

D

Lawford Heath
Industrial Estate

5

A4071

Caws

Lawford Heath

COVENTRY ROAD

Ca

The
Ryelands

E

Lawford Heat
ne

F

74

G

H

The
Crescent

Potford's Dam
Farm

66
View Road

The Green

Back
Lane

A **B** **C** **D**

A428 RUGBY ROAD **50**

Briars Close

Paynes Lane

Somers Rd

St Oswalds
C of E First
School

1

Bilton
Lane

Wynter
Rd

St
Oswald
Wy

Cemetery

Somers
Road

vford Hill
m

2

Bilton

Henry Hinde
Middle School

Wilson Cl

Keys Drive

Freemantle
Road

Madden
Place

Anson
Cl

Addison

Kennedy
Drive

Evans Road

Mulberry Road

Apple
Gv

Birch Dr

Rowan Dr

Larch
Cl

Dreyer Close

Road

Road

1

2

Hardy

Blackwood Av

Beatty
Drive

Hood's
Way

May La

Lane

Elder
Cl

Lilac Cl

Lestock
Close

Barrington
Road

Blake

1

Nelson
Way

Collingwood Av

Pear Tree
Way

Acorn
Dr

1

2

Cowan

Frobisher

Keppel

2

Hillfield
Road

Wheatfield Avenue

Spicer

3

3

Henry Hinde
First School

Ditton Cl

Plexfield Rd

3

65

Lawford

Montgomery
Drive

Pipewell
Pl

Beech Dr

Carlton
Rd

4 **5**

6

Church Walk

Gables

Pool

4

Lane

3

Doctors
Surgery

PO

THE GREEN

Crescent
School

Orchard
Way

Selb

D1
1 Oswald Wy

Cawston Grange
Farm

Winwick
Pl

Stocks
Ct

1

Barton
Rd

5

MAIN STREET

Magnet Lane

2

Bilton County
First School

St Mark's Av

1

1

1

Bilton

COVENTRY ROAD

Lime Tree Avenue

Alwyn Road

St Mark's Av

Dalkeith Avenue

Beswick Gardens

Hampden
Way

Bawnmore Road

Cawston

A4071

Cawston Lane

Scots
Close

Highgrove

Martin
Lane

Rugby High
School

A **B** **C** **D**

Cawston
House

75

Longford
Road

Cymbeline

Duncan
Drive

Heron
Cl

Bilton C
Middle

Bilton C

COVENTRY ROAD

51

E
E1
1 Dryden Pl
2 Dryden Wk

F

G

Street names for this grid square are listed at the back of the index
E3

H

E4
1 Bathurst Cl
2 Cherry Gv
3 Laburnum Gv

I

F1
1 Alfred St
2 Bennett St
3 Easy La
4 Levy Cl
5 Ltl Pennington St
6 Parnell Cl
7 Pennington Ms
8 Pennington St
9 Round St
10 Schoolfield Gv
11 Stephen St
12 Torrance Rd

2

F2
1 Westfield Rd

3

68

F3
1 Wentworth Rd
2 Westbourne Gv

4

F4
1 Overslade Mnr Dr

F5
1 Goldsmith Av

5

Spring Farm

G1
1 Bank St
2 Bloxam Pl
3 Drury La
4 Eastfield Pl
5 Elborow St
6 Evreux Wy
7 Henry St
8 Lawford Rd
9 Little Church St
10 Little Elborow St
11 Pennington St

E
H1
1 Castle Ms
2 Murraylan Cl

F

G
G2
1 Bilton Rd
2 John Thwaites Cl
3 L Sheriff St
4 Russelsheim Wy

H

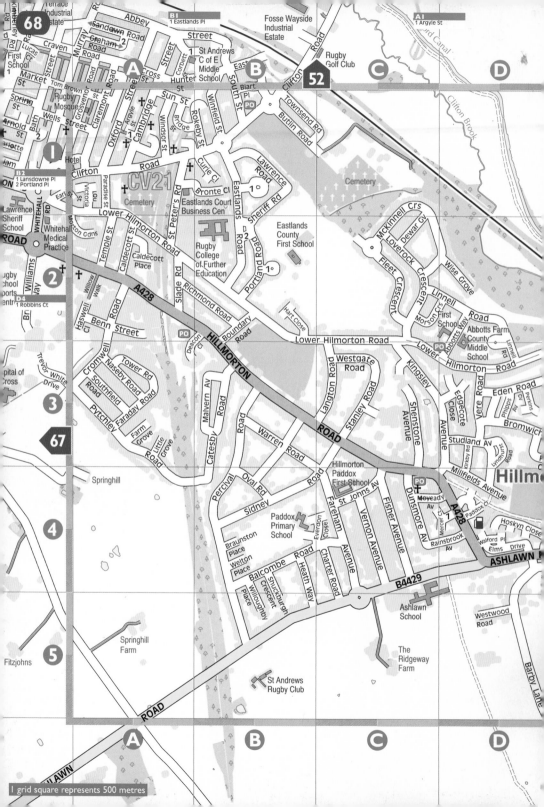

E4
1 Deane Pde

F4
1 Harrison Cl
2 Palmer's Cl

E **F** 53 **G** **H**

I

2

3

4

5

Home Farm

Oxford Canal

The Locks

Waverley Road

Kent

The Lane

Robert Hill Close
Pine Grove

Brindley Road

Jenkins Rd

Jackson Rd

Lever Rd

Wigston Rd

School Gdns

School Street

Coton

Gainsborough Crts

Constable Road

Fox Cl

Landseer

Reynolds

Bonnington Close

Turner Cl

Lower Street

Watts Lane

Deane Road

Wesley Rd

Bell Wk

Fenwick Dr

Roper Cl

Hillmorton First School

Mellor Rd

1

Packwood Av

Browning Road

Miers Road

Deerings Road

Rathbone Cl

Gatehouse Cl

Gatehouse Cl

Cemetery

Horne Close

Archer's Spinney

PO

HIGH STREET A428

Hotel

Duffy Pl

Barley Cl

Vale

Cockerill's Meadow

Chamberlain Road

Bucknill Crescent

Astley Place

Killworth Road

Foresters Place

Eastwood Grove

Leys Road

Lennon Cl

CRICK

ROAD A428

B4038 **KILSBY LANE**

glish artyrs C School

Moat Farm Drive

Oxford Canal Path

Oxford Canal Path

E **F** **G** **H**

Ⓐ Ⓑ Ⓒ Ⓓ

Honiley Farm
Business Park

A4177

54

HONILEY ROAD

1

Hotel

2

Manor Lane

Honiley

✝

3

Lane

4

PO

Haseley Knob

5

Beausale

Butlers
End

Barracks La

Ⓐ Ⓑ Ⓒ Ⓓ

Kites Ne

ood

I grid square represents 500 metres

Little Chase
Farm

E

Warriors Lodge
Farm

F

55

G

H

East
Far

Chase   Lane

I

Pleasance Farm

Chase Wood

2

Grove Farm

3

72

4

Inchford   Brook

Fernhill
Farm

Fernwood
Farm

5

Rouncil Lane

E

F

G

H

1 grid

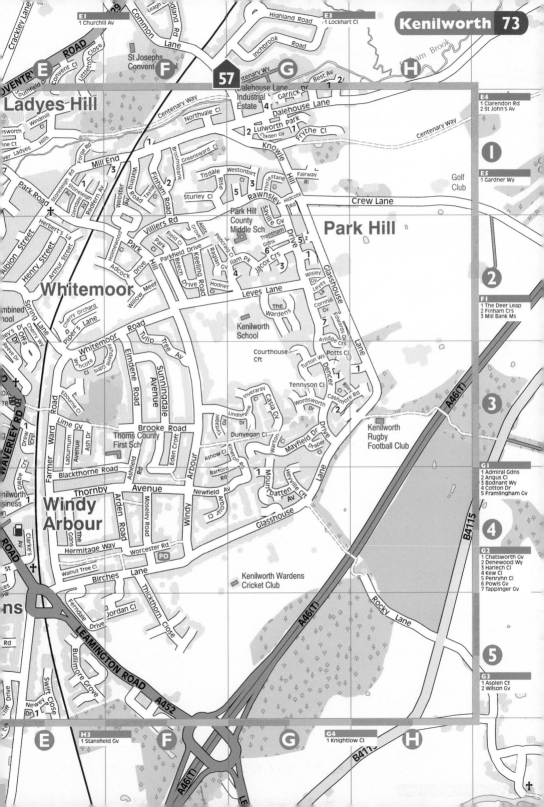

Crackley Lane

COVENTRY ROAD

1 Churchill Av E1

Highland Road

1 Lockhart Cl E3

Leigh Rd

Woodland Rd

Common Lane

Littleton Close

Convent Cl

St Josephs Convent F1

Inchbrook Road

Centenary Wy

57

Dalehouse Lane

Best Av G

Nein Brook

1 Clarendon Rd E4
2 St John's Av

Ladyes Hill

Southfield Dr

Windmill

Ladyes Hills

Forge Rd

Mill End

Stoneleigh Rd

Glendale Av

Stoneleigh Av

Redfern Av

Park Road

Watling Road

Webster

Taylor Cl

Finham Road

Centenary Way

Northvale Cl

Industrial Estate

Dalehouse Lane

Lulworth Park

Virden Gv

Frythe Cl

Knowle

Broomybank

Greensward Cl

Tisdale

Westonbirt Cl

Rawnsley Dr

Firestane Rd

Hidcote Rd

Fairway Ri

Savile Gv

Crew Lane

Golf Club

1 Gardner Wy E5

I

2

1 The Deer Leap F1
2 Finham Crs
3 Mill Bank Ms

Park Hill

Park Hill County Middle Sch

Trentham Gdns

Glasshouse Drive

Wisley Gv

Leyes

Cornhill

Edwards Gv

Arlidge Crs

Potts Cl

Lane

Whitemoor

Albion Street

Henry Street

Arthur Street

Herbert's La

Holmewood

Villiers Rd

Park Hill

Adcock

Park Drive

Field Cl

Alliott Grove

Parkfield Drive

Keeling Road

Beech Drive

Raglan Cl

Hodnet

Illam Pk

Jacox Crs

Leyes Lane

The Wardens

Kenilworth School

Courthouse Cft

Turton Wy

Denler

Tennyson Cl

Wordsworth Dr

Cashmore Rd

Riley

Kenilworth Rugby Football Club

A46(T)

B4115

3

1 Admiral Gdns G1
2 Angus Cl
3 Bodnant Wy
4 Cotton Dr
5 Framlingham Gv

Spring Lane

Combined School

Reeve Dr

Offa

Cherry Orchard

Piper's Lane

Whitemoor Road

Whitemoor Cl

Withcote Cl

Ashgrove

Elmdene Road

Tulip Tree Av

Sunningdale Avenue

Brooke Road

Inveraray Cl

Casia Cv

Lindisfarne Dr

Dunvegan Cl

Warton

Mayfield Drive

Draper

Glasshouse Lane

4

1 Chatsworth Gv G2
2 Denewood Wy
3 Harlech Cl
4 Kew Cl
5 Penrhyn Cl
6 Powis Gv
7 Tappinger Gv

WAVERLEY RD

Glebe Crs

Drew Cl

Lime Gv

Ward Road

Farmer Road

Laburnum Avenue

Blackthorne Road

Ebourne Cl

Ash Dr

Thorns County First Sch

Ashfield Rd

Eden Croft

Windy Arbour

Barford Rd

Ashow Cl

Kineton Rd

Newfield AV

Arbour

Mountbatten AV

Heyville Cft

5

Thornby Avenue

Arden Road

Moseley Road

Worcester Rd

PO

The Gdns

Hermitage Way

Walnut Tree Cl

Birches Lane

Thickthorn Close

Jordan Cl

Kenilworth Wardens Cricket Club

Rocky Lane

1 Asplen Ct G3
2 Wilson Gv

Ferndale Drive

Bullimore Grove

LEAMINGTON ROAD

A452

Swift Close

Newel Cl

Cliff Drive

A46(T)

Alderman's Green ... 16 C4
Allesley ... 23 F3
Ash Green ... 15 E2
Baginton ... 59 H2
Balsall Common ... 38 C1
Barnacle ... 17 H2
Beausale ... 70 C5
Bedworth ... 6 B5
Bedworth Heath ... 5 G4
Beechwood ... 39 F3
Bell Green ... 26 B3
Benton Green ... 31 E4
Berkswell ... 30 D3
Bilton ... 66 C5
Binley ... 45 E1
Binley Woods ... 46 A2
Black Bank ... 6 A4
Bradnock's Marsh ... 29 F3
Brandon ... 46 D4
Bretford ... 48 A2
Brownshill Green ... 23 G2
Brownsover ... 52 A2
Burton Green ... 40 A5
Canley ... 41 G3
Carol Green ... 39 F1
Catchems Corner ... 39 E4
Cawston ... 66 A5
Chapel Fields ... 34 A4
Chapel Green ... 12 A1
Cheylesmore ... 43 G2
Church End ... 36 C3
Church Lawford ... 48 D4
Clifton upon Dunsmore ... 53 E4
Coalpit Field ... 6 D4
Collycroft ... 6 B1
Corley Moor ... 12 C1
Coundon ... 24 A4
Court House Green ... 26 A4
Coventry ... 34 C3

Crackley ... 57 F5
Dunchurch ... 75 H4
Dunsmore ... 53 H4
Earlsdon ... 34 C5
Eastcote ... 28 A3
Eaves Green ... 21 F1
Edgwick ... 25 G3
Exhall ... 16 B1
Finham ... 58 D1
Flint's Green ... 31 F1
Foleshill ... 25 H3
Four Oaks ... 30 D1
Foxford ... 16 A4
Gibbet Hill ... 58 A2
Goodyers End ... 5 E4
Gosford Green ... 3 K4
Great Heath ... 25 G4
Green Lane ... 42 C4
Hall Green ... 16 B5
Hampton in Arden ... 18 D5
Harvest Hill ... 22 B1
Haseley Knob ... 70 B4
Hawkesbury ... 16 C2
Hawkes End ... 23 E1
Henley Green ... 26 D3
Hillfields ... 3 F1
Hillmorton ... 68 D4
Hockley ... 31 H2
Holbrooks ... 15 E5
Hollyberry End ... 12 B4
Hollyhurst ... 7 E5
Honiley ... 70 D2
Hook End ... 28 D1
Kenilworth ... 72 C4
Keresley ... 14 B4
Keresley Newlands ... 14 D2
Kings Hill ... 58 D2
King's Newnham ... 49 E2
Kinwalsey ... 11 F1

Kirby Corner ... 41 E3
Ladyes Hill ... 73 E1
Lawford Heath ... 65 F5
Lime Tree Park ... 33 E5
Little Heath ... 25 H2
Little Lawford ... 50 A2
Little Packington ... 8 D2
Lodge Green ... 10 D5
Longford ... 15 H4
Long Lawford ... 49 H4
Lower Eastern Green ... 32 C3
Lower Stoke ... 36 A5
Manor House ... 26 C1
Marston ... 47 G4
Meer End ... 54 C3
Meriden ... 20 D2
Middle Bickenhill ... 8 C5
Middle Stoke ... 36 A3
Mount Pleasant ... 6 A2
Neal's Green ... 15 F2
New Bilton ... 66 D2
Newbold on Avon ... 51 E4
Outwoods ... 10 B2
Overslade ... 67 E3
Park Hill ... 73 G2
Pickford ... 22 C3
Pickford Green ... 22 B4
Pinkett's Booth ... 22 B3
Pinley ... 44 A2
Potter's Green ... 27 F2
Radford ... 25 E5
Reeves Green ... 39 G1
Rowley's Green ... 15 G4
Rugby ... 67 H3
Ryton-on-Dunsmore ... 61 H2
St Johns ... 72 D5
Spon End ... 34 C4
The Spring ... 56 D5
Stivichall ... 43 E4

Stoke ... 36
Stoke Aldermoor ... 44
Stoke Heath ... 26
Stonebridge ... 18
Thurlaston ... 74
Tile Hill ... 32
Toft ... 75
Tollbar End ... 44
Upper Eastern Green ... 22
Upper Stoke ... 36
Walsal End ... 28
Walsgrave on Sowe ... 27
Weston in Arden ... 7
Westwood Heath ... 40
Whitemoor ... 73
Whitley ... 43
Whitmore Park ... 24
Whoberley ... 33
Willenhall ... 44
Windy Arbour ... 73
Wolston ... 63
Wood End ... 26
Woodway Park ... 27
Wootton Green ... 29
Wyken ... 36

USING THE STREET INDEX

Street names are listed alphabetically. Each street name is followed by its postal town or area locality, the Postcode District, the page number, and the reference to the square in which the name is found.

Example: **Abbey End** *KNWTH* CV8.................**72** D3 🔟

Some entries are followed by a number in a blue box. This number indicates the location of the street within the referenced grid square. The full street name is listed at the side of the map page.

GENERAL ABBREVIATIONS

ACC	ACCESS	CSWY	CAUSEWAY	GND	GROUND	MEM	MEMORIA
ALY	ALLEY	CT	COURT	GRA	GRANGE	MKT	MARKE
AP	APPROACH	CTRL	CENTRAL	GRG	GARAGE	MKTS	MARKE
AR	ARCADE	CTS	COURTS	GT	GREAT	ML	MAI
ASS	ASSOCIATION	CTYD	COURTYARD	GTWY	GATEWAY	ML	MII
AV	AVENUE	CUTT	CUTTINGS	GV	GROVE	MNR	MANO
BCH	BEACH	CV	COVE	HGR	HIGHER	MS	MEW
BLDS	BUILDINGS	CYN	CANYON	HL	HILL	MSN	MISSIO
BND	BEND	DEPT	DEPARTMENT	HLS	HILLS	MT	MOUN
BNK	BANK	DL	DALE	HO	HOUSE	MTN	MOUNTAI
BR	BRIDGE	DM	DAM	HOL	HOLLOW	MTS	MOUNTAIN
BRK	BROOK	DR	DRIVE	HOSP	HOSPITAL	MUS	MUSEU
BTM	BOTTOM	DRO	DROVE	HRB	HARBOUR	MWY	MOTORWA
BUS	BUSINESS	DRY	DRIVEWAY	HTH	HEATH	N	NORT
BVD	BOULEVARD	DWGS	DWELLINGS	HTS	HEIGHTS	NE	NORTH EAS
BY	BYPASS	E	EAST	HVN	HAVEN	NW	NORTH WES
CATH	CATHEDRAL	EMB	EMBANKMENT	HWY	HIGHWAY	O/P	OVERPAS
CEM	CEMETERY	EMBY	EMBASSY	IMP	IMPERIAL	OFF	OFFIC
CEN	CENTRE	ESP	ESPLANADE	IN	INLET	ORCH	ORCHAR
CFT	CROFT	EST	ESTATE	IND EST	INDUSTRIAL ESTATE	OV	OVA
CH	CHURCH	EX	EXCHANGE	INF	INFIRMARY	PAL	PALAC
CHA	CHASE	EXPY	EXPRESSWAY	INFO	INFORMATION	PAS	PASSAC
CHYD	CHURCHYARD	EXT	EXTENSION	INT	INTERCHANGE	PAV	PAVILIO
CIR	CIRCLE	F/O	FLYOVER	IS	ISLAND	PDE	PARAD
CIRC	CIRCUS	FC	FOOTBALL CLUB	JCT	JUNCTION	PH	PUBLIC HOUS
CL	CLOSE	FK	FORK	JTY	JETTY	PK	PAR
CLFS	CLIFFS	FLD	FIELD	KG	KING	PKWY	PARKWA
CMP	CAMP	FLDS	FIELDS	KNL	KNOLL	PL	PLAC
CNR	CORNER	FLS	FALLS	L	LAKE	PLN	PLAI
CO	COUNTY	FLS	FLATS	LA	LANE	PLNS	PLAIN
COLL	COLLEGE	FM	FARM	LDG	LODGE	PLZ	PLAZ
COM	COMMON	FT	FORT	LGT	LIGHT	POL	POLICE STATIO
COMM	COMMISSION	FWY	FREEWAY	LK	LOCK	PR	PRINC
CON	CONVENT	FY	FERRY	LKS	LAKES	PREC	PRECINC
COT	COTTAGE	GA	GATE	LNDG	LANDING	PREP	PREPARATOR
COTS	COTTAGES	GAL	GALLERY	LTL	LITTLE	PRIM	PRIMAR
CP	CAPE	GDN	GARDEN	LWR	LOWER	PROM	PROMENAD
CPS	COPSE	GDNS	GARDENS	MAG	MAGISTRATE	PRS	PRINCES
CR	CREEK	GLD	GLADE	MAN	MANSIONS	PRT	PO
CREM	CREMATORIUM	GLN	GLEN	MD	MEAD	PT	POI
CRS	CRESCENT	GN	GREEN	MDW	MEADOWS	PTH	PA

?Z ......PIAZZA
?D ......QUADRANT
?U ......QUEEN
?Y ......QUAY
? ......RIVER
?BT ......ROUNDABOUT
?D ......ROAD
?DG ......RIDGE
?EP ......REPUBLIC
?ES ......RESERVOIR
?FC ......RUGBY FOOTBALL CLUB
?I ......RISE
?P ......RAMP
?W ......ROW
? ......SOUTH
?CH ......SCHOOL

SE ......SOUTH EAST
SER ......SERVICE AREA
SH ......SHORE
SHOP ......SHOPPING
SKWY ......SKYWAY
SMT ......SUMMIT
SOC ......SOCIETY
SP ......SPUR
SPR ......SPRING
SQ ......SQUARE
ST ......STREET
STN ......STATION
STR ......STREAM
STRD ......STRAND
SW ......SOUTH WEST
TDG ......TRADING

TER ......TERRACE
THWY ......THROUGHWAY
TNL ......TUNNEL
TOLL ......TOLLWAY
TPK ......TURNPIKE
TR ......TRACK
TRL ......TRAIL
TWR ......TOWER
U/P ......UNDERPASS
UNI ......UNIVERSITY
UPR ......UPPER
V ......VALE
VA ......VALLEY
VIAD ......VIADUCT
VIL ......VILLA
VIS ......VISTA

VLG ......VILLAGE
VLS ......VILLAS
VW ......VIEW
W ......WEST
WD ......WOOD
WHF ......WHARF
WK ......WALK
WKS ......WALKS
WLS ......WELLS
WY ......WAY
YD ......YARD
YHA ......YOUTH HOSTEL

POSTCODE TOWNS AND AREA ABBREVIATIONS

BDWTH ......Bedworth
BHAMNEC ......Birmingham N.E.C.
CHWD/FDBR/MGN ......Chelmsley Wood/Fordbridge/Marston Green
COV ......Coventry
COVE ......Coventry east

COVN ......Coventry north
COVS ......Coventry south
COVW ......Coventry west
CSHL/WTROR ......Coleshill/Water Orton
DOR/KN ......Dorridge/Knowle
HIA/OLT ......Hampton in Arden/Olton

KNWTH ......Kenilworth
NUNW/HART ......Nuneaton west/Hartshill
RCOVN/BALC/EX ......Rural Coventry north/Balsall Common/Exhall
RRUGBY ......Rural Rugby
RUGBYN/HIL ......Rugby north/Hillmorton

RUGBYS/DCH ......Rugby south/Dunchurch
TLHL/CAN ......Tile Hill/Canley
WWCK ......Rural Warwick/Wellesbourne

Index - streets

Abb - Ban

A

Abberton Wy TLHL/CAN CV4 ...... 57 H1
Abbeydale Cl COVS CV3 ...... 37 F3
Abbey End KNWTH CV8 ...... 72 D5 ■
Abbey Hl KNWTH CV8 ...... 72 D3
Abbey Rd COVS CV3 ...... 44 A3
Abbey St RUGBYN/HIL CV21 ...... 52 A5
Abbey Wy COVS CV3 ...... 43 H3
Abbotsbury Cl COVE CV2 ...... 37 G2
Abbotts La COV CV1 ...... 2 B2
Abbotts Wk COVS CV3 ...... 46 A2
Abbotts Wy RUGBYN/HIL CV21 ...... 68 D3
Abercorn Rd COVW CV5 ...... 34 B4 ■
Aberdeen Cl COVW CV5 ...... 33 E1
Abergavenny Wk COVS CV3 ...... 45 F3
Acacia Av COV CV1 ...... 3 G6
Acacia Crs BDWTH CV12 ...... 6 D2
Acacia Gv RUGBYN/HIL CV21 ...... 51 G5
Achal Cl COVN CV6 ...... 25 H1
Achilles Rd COVN CV6 ...... 26 A5
Acorn Cl BDWTH CV12 ...... 5 E5
   KNWTH CV8 ...... 58 D5
Acorn Rd RUGBYS/DCH CV22 ...... 66 B3
Acorn St COVS CV3 ...... 44 B1
Adam Rd COVN CV6 ...... 26 A4 ■
Adams St RUGBYN/HIL CV21 ...... 67 E1
Adare Dr COV CV3 ...... 43 E1
Adcock Dr KNWTH CV8 ...... 73 F2
Addenbrooke Rd
   RCOVN/BALC/EX CV7 ...... 14 C2 ■
Adderley St COV CV1 ...... 35 G2
Addison Rd COVN CV6 ...... 24 C3
   RUGBYS/DCH CV22 ...... 66 D2
Adelaide St COV CV1 ...... 35 G2 ■
Adkinson Av RUGBYS/DCH CV22 ...... 75 C4
Admiral Gdns KNWTH CV8 ...... 73 G1 ■
Agincourt Rd COVS CV3 ...... 43 G3 ■
Ainsbury Rd COVW CV5 ...... 42 A1
Ainsdale Cl COVE CV2 ...... 16 B4
Aintree Cl BDWTH CV12 ...... 6 B1
   COVN CV6 ...... 35 G1
Alandale Av COVW CV5 ...... 32 C2
Alan Higgs Wy TLHL/CAN CV4 ...... 40 A2
Albany Rd COVW CV5 ...... 34 C5
Albert Crs COVN CV6 ...... 14 D5
Albert Rd COVW CV5 ...... 21 G3
Albert Sq RUGBYN/HIL CV21 ...... 67 H1
Albert St COV CV1 ...... 3 G1
   RUGBYN/HIL CV21 ...... 67 G1
Albion St KNWTH CV8 ...... 73 E2
Aldbourne Rd COV CV1 ...... 35 E1
Aldbury Ri COVW CV5 ...... 33 G2
Alder La RCOVN/BALC/EX CV7 ...... 38 C4
Alderman's Green Rd COVN CV6 ...... 16 B5
Alder Meadow Cl COVN CV6 ...... 15 F4 ■
Alderminster Rd COVW CV5 ...... 33 E2
Aldermoor La COVS CV3 ...... 44 A1
Alderney Cl COVN CV6 ...... 24 D1
Aldrich Av COV CV4 ...... 32 C4
Aldin Wy TLHL/CAN CV4 ...... 41 H4
Alexander Rd BDWTH CV12 ...... 6 C2
lexandra Rd COV CV1 ...... 3 J1 ■

   RUGBYN/HIL CV21 ...... 51 H5
Alex Grierson Cl COVS CV3 ...... 45 E2
Alfall Rd COVE CV2 ...... 36 B1
Alfred Green Cl
   RUGBYS/DCH CV22 ...... 67 G2
Alfred Rd COV CV1 ...... 35 H2
Alfred St RUGBYN/HIL CV21 ...... 67 F1 ■
Alfriston Rd COVS CV3 ...... 43 E5
Alice Cl BDWTH CV12 ...... 5 H4
Alison Sq COVN CV6 ...... 16 B4 ■
Allan Rd COVN CV6 ...... 34 B2
Allans Cl RRUGBY CV23 ...... 53 E4
Allans La RRUGBY CV23 ...... 53 E4
Allard Wy COVS CV3 ...... 44 C2
Allerton Cl COVE CV2 ...... 37 E4
Allesley Cft COVW CV5 ...... 23 E5
Allesley Hall Dr COVW CV5 ...... 33 G1
Allesley Old Rd COV CV1 ...... 34 C4 ■
   COVW CV5 ...... 33 G1
Allesley Rd RUGBYN/HIL CV21 ...... 51 F3
Alliance Wy COVE CV2 ...... 36 A1
Allied Cl COVN CV6 ...... 25 F1 ■
Allitt Gv KNWTH CV8 ...... 73 F2
All Saints La COV CV1 ...... 3 H3
All Saints Rd BDWTH CV12 ...... 5 H4 ■
Alma St COV CV1 ...... 3 G3
Almond Gv RUGBYN/HIL CV21 ...... 51 E2
Almond Tree Av COVE CV2 ...... 26 C1
Alpine Ct KNWTH CV8 ...... 73 E1
Alpine Ri COVS CV3 ...... 42 C4
Alspath La COVW CV5 ...... 32 D2
Alspath Rd RCOVN/BALC/EX CV7 ...... 20 C2
Alton Cl COVE CV2 ...... 26 D1
Alum Cl COVN CV6 ...... 25 F3
Alverstone Rd COVE CV2 ...... 36 A2
Alvin Cl COVS CV3 ...... 37 F5
Alwyn Rd RUGBYS/DCH CV22 ...... 66 C5
Ambler Gv COVE CV2 ...... 36 C3
Ambleside COVE CV2 ...... 27 E1
   RUGBYN/HIL CV21 ...... 52 B2
Ambrose Cl RUGBYN/HIL CV21 ...... 52 A3 ■
Amersham Cl COVW CV5 ...... 33 F2 ■
Amherst Rd KNWTH CV8 ...... 72 C1
Amos Jacques Rd BDWTH CV12 ...... 6 A1
Amy Cl COVN CV6 ...... 15 H4
Anchorway Rd COVS CV3 ...... 42 D5
Anderson Av RUGBYS/DCH CV22 ...... 67 G4
Anderton Rd BDWTH CV12 ...... 5 E4
   COVE CV2 ...... 16 B3 ■
Angela Av COVE CV2 ...... 27 E2
Anglesey Cl COVW CV5 ...... 23 F4
Angless Wy KNWTH CV8 ...... 72 D4 ■
Angus Cl COVW CV5 ...... 33 E2
   KNWTH CV8 ...... 73 G1 ■
Anker Dr RRUGBY CV23 ...... 50 B4
Anne Crs COVS CV3 ...... 44 C4
Ansells Dr COVN CV6 ...... 16 A3
Anson Cl RUGBYS/DCH CV22 ...... 66 C2
Anson Wy COVE CV2 ...... 27 F3
Ansty Rd COVE CV2 ...... 36 C2
   COVE CV2 ...... 36 C2
Anthony Wy COVE CV2 ...... 36 C4
Antrim Cl COVW CV5 ...... 23 E4
Applecross Cl TLHL/CAN CV4 ...... 40 D3
Appledore Dr COVW CV5 ...... 32 D1
Apple Gv RUGBYS/DCH CV22 ...... 66 B2
The Arboretum TLHL/CAN CV4 ...... 57 H1

Arbour Cl KNWTH CV8 ...... 73 F4
Arbury Av BDWTH CV12 ...... 6 A2
   COVN CV6 ...... 25 G1
Archer Rd KNWTH CV8 ...... 72 C4
Archers Spinney
   RUGBYN/HIL CV21 ...... 69 F4
Archery Rd RCOVN/BALC/EX CV7 ...... 20 B2
Arches La RUGBYN/HIL CV21 ...... 52 A4
Arch Rd COVE CV2 ...... 37 E1
Arden Cl RCOVN/BALC/EX CV7 ...... 20 C2
   RCOVN/BALC/EX CV7 ...... 38 B2
   RUGBYS/DCH CV22 ...... 75 H2
Arden Rd KNWTH CV8 ...... 73 F4
Arden St COVW CV5 ...... 34 B5
Argyle St RUGBYN/HIL CV21 ...... 68 A1 ■
Argyll St COVE CV2 ...... 36 A3
Ariel Wy RUGBYS/DCH CV22 ...... 75 H1
Arkle Dr COVE CV2 ...... 27 F4
Arlidge Crs KNWTH CV8 ...... 73 G2
Armarna Dr COVW CV5 ...... 21 H3 ■
Armfield St COVN CV6 ...... 26 A3
Armorial Rd COVS CV3 ...... 42 D3
Armscott Rd COVE CV2 ...... 26 C5
   COVE CV2 ...... 36 C1
Armson Rd RCOVN/BALC/EX CV7 ...... 6 A4
Armstrong Av COVS CV3 ...... 36 A5
Armstrong Cl
   RUGBYS/DCH CV22 ...... 67 E3 ■
Arne Rd COVE CV2 ...... 27 G5
Arnhem Cnr COVS CV3 ...... 44 D3
Arnold Av COVS CV3 ...... 43 E4
Arnold St RUGBYN/HIL CV21 ...... 67 H1
Arnside Cl COV CV1 ...... 3 G1
Arthingworth Cl COVS CV3 ...... 37 G5
Arthur St COV CV1 ...... 35 F2 ■
   KNWTH CV8 ...... 73 E2
Arundel Rd COVS CV3 ...... 43 F3
Asbury Rd RCOVN/BALC/EX CV7 ...... 38 B4
Ascot Cl BDWTH CV12 ...... 6 B1
   COVS CV3 ...... 44 C3
Ashbridge Rd COVW CV5 ...... 33 G2
Ashburton Rd COVE CV2 ...... 27 E4
Ashby Cl COVS CV3 ...... 45 F1
Ashcombe Dr TLHL/CAN CV4 ...... 32 D3
Ash Ct RUGBYS/DCH CV22 ...... 67 E5
Ashcroft Cl COVE CV2 ...... 27 G3 ■
Ashcroft Wy
   RCOVN/BALC/EX CV7 ...... 27 H1
Ashdale Cl COVS CV3 ...... 46 C2
Ashdene Gdns KNWTH CV8 ...... 73 F3
Ashdown Cl COVS CV3 ...... 44 D1
Ash Dr KNWTH CV8 ...... 73 E3
Ashfield Av TLHL/CAN CV4 ...... 32 B5
Ashfield Rd KNWTH CV8 ...... 73 F4
Ashford Dr BDWTH CV12 ...... 6 A2 ■
Ashfurlong Cl
   RCOVN/BALC/EX CV7 ...... 38 B3 ■
Ash Green La
   RCOVN/BALC/EX CV7 ...... 15 E2
Ash Gv RCOVN/BALC/EX CV7 ...... 15 E1
Ashington Gv COVS CV3 ...... 44 A4
Ashington Rd BDWTH CV12 ...... 5 E4
Ashlawn Rd RUGBYN/HIL CV21 ...... 68 D4
Ashley Wy RCOVN/BALC/EX CV7 ...... 38 B2
Ashman Av RRUGBY CV23 ...... 50 B4
Ashmore Rd COVN CV6 ...... 34 D2 ■

Ashorne Cl COVE CV2 ...... 26 C1 ■
   COVE CV2 ...... 26 D1 ■
Ashow Cl KNWTH CV8 ...... 73 F3
Ash Priors Cl TLHL/CAN CV4 ...... 33 F4
Ash Tree Av TLHL/CAN CV4 ...... 33 E4
Ashurst Cl COVN CV6 ...... 16 B3 ■
Ashwood Av COVN CV6 ...... 34 B1 ■
Aspen Cl TLHL/CAN CV4 ...... 32 B5 ■
Asplen Ct KNWTH CV8 ...... 73 G3 ■
Asra Cl COVE CV2 ...... 35 H2
Assheton Cl
   RUGBYS/DCH CV22 ...... 66 C4 ■
Asthill Cft COVS CV3 ...... 2 C7
Asthill Gv COVS CV3 ...... 43 E1
Astley Av COVN CV6 ...... 25 G1
Astley Pl RUGBYN/HIL CV21 ...... 69 F5
Aston Rd COVW CV5 ...... 34 B5
Atherston Pl TLHL/CAN CV4 ...... 41 H3 ■
Athol Rd COVE CV2 ...... 27 G5
Attoxhall Rd COVE CV2 ...... 37 E2
Attwood Crs COVE CV2 ...... 26 C5
Augustus Rd COV CV1 ...... 3 J1
Austin Dr COVN CV6 ...... 26 A4
Avenue Rd KNWTH CV8 ...... 72 B1
   RUGBYN/HIL CV21 ...... 51 E5
The Avenue COVS CV3 ...... 44 A3
Avocet Cl COVN CV6 ...... 26 B1
Avondale Rd COVW CV5 ...... 42 C1
   KNWTH CV8 ...... 46 D4
Avonmere RUGBYN/HIL CV21 ...... 51 E3
Avon Rd KNWTH CV8 ...... 72 C4
Avon St COVE CV2 ...... 36 B1
   RRUGBY CV23 ...... 52 C5
   RUGBYN/HIL CV21 ...... 51 G5 ■
Awson St COVN CV6 ...... 25 H5
Axholme Rd COVE CV2 ...... 37 E2
Aylesford St COV CV1 ...... 35 G2
Aynho Cl COVW CV5 ...... 33 E3

B

Babbacombe Rd COVS CV3 ...... 43 F4
Bablake Cl COVN CV6 ...... 24 B3
Back La RCOVN/BALC/EX CV7 ...... 30 D1
   RRUGBY CV23 ...... 50 A5
Badby Leys RUGBYS/DCH CV22 ...... 67 F5
Badger Rd COVS CV3 ...... 44 D1
Baffin Cl RUGBYS/DCH CV22 ...... 67 E3 ■
Baginton Rd COVS CV3 ...... 42 D3
Bagshaw Cl KNWTH CV8 ...... 61 G3
Bailey's La RRUGBY CV23 ...... 60 A1
Bakehouse La RUGBYN/HIL CV21 ...... 67 F1
Bakers La COVW CV5 ...... 34 A4
Baker St COVN CV6 ...... 16 B2
Bakewell Cl COVS CV3 ...... 45 F1
Balcombe Rd RUGBYS/DCH CV22 ...... 68 B4
Baldwin Cft COVN CV6 ...... 26 B2
Ballantine Rd COVN CV6 ...... 24 D5
Ballingham Cl TLHL/CAN CV4 ...... 33 E4
Balliol Rd COVE CV2 ...... 36 B2
Balmoral Cl COVE CV2 ...... 27 E5
Balsall St East
   RCOVN/BALC/EX CV7 ...... 38 A4
Bankside Cl COVS CV3 ...... 43 H3
Banks Rd COVN CV6 ...... 34 C1

Bank St *RUGBYN/HIL* CV21 .... 67 G1 ▯
Banner La *TLHL/CAN* CV4 .... 32 B3
Bantam Gv *COVN* CV6 .... 14 C5
Bantock Rd *TLHL/CAN* CV4 .... 32 C4
Barbican Ri *COVE* CV2 .... 37 E4
Barbridge Rd *BDWTH* CV12 .... 7 H3
Barby La *RUGBYN/HIL* CV21 ...... 68 D5
Barby Rd *RUGBYS/DCH* CV22 ..... 67 G3
Barford Cl *COVS* CV3 .... 44 D1 ▯
Barford Rd *KNWTH* CV8 .... 73 F4
Barkers' Butts La *COVN* CV6 ...... 34 B1
Barley Cl *RUGBYN/HIL* CV21 ...... 69 E4
The Barley Lea *COVS* CV3 .... 44 B1
Barlow Rd *COVE* CV2 .... 16 D5
Barnack Av *COVS* CV3 .... 42 D4
Barnfield Av *COVW* CV5 .... 32 D1 ▯
Barnstaple Cl *COVW* CV5 .... 32 D1 ▯
Barnwell Cl *RUGBYS/DCH* CV22 .. 75 C3
Baron's Cft *COVS* CV3 .... 43 G2
Baron's Field Rd *COVS* CV3 ...... 43 F2
Barracks La *RWWCK/WEL* CV35 .. 70 C5
Barracks Wy *COV* CV1 .... 2 D4 ▯
Barras Gn *COVE* CV2 .... 36 A2
Barras La *COV* CV1 .... 2 A3
Barretts La *RCOVN/BALC/EX* CV7 .. 38 C3
Barrington Rd
  RUGBYS/DCH CV22 .... 66 C2
Barrow Cl *COVE* CV2 .... 27 H5
Barrowfield La *KNWTH* CV8 .... 72 D5
Barrow Rd *KNWTH* CV8 .... 72 D3
Barston Cl *COVN* CV6 .... 16 A5
Barston La *HIA/OLT* B92 .... 28 D5
Bartlett Cl *COVN* CV6 .... 25 G1
Barton Rd *BDWTH* CV12 .... 6 B1
  COV CV6 .... 25 H1 ▯
  RUGBYS/DCH CV22 .... 66 D4
Barton's Meadow *COVE* CV2 ...... 36 B1
Basford Brook Dr *COVN* CV6 ...... 15 H3
Basley Wy *COVW* CV5 .... 15 F4
Bassett Rd *COVN* CV6 .... 34 C1
Bateman's Acre South
  COVN CV6 .... 34 C2 ▯
Bates Rd *COVW* CV5 .... 42 A2
Bath St *COV* CV1 .... 3 F1
  RUGBYN/HIL CV21 .... 67 H1
Bathurst Cl *RUGBYS/DCH* CV22 .. 67 E4 ▯
Bathurst Rd *COVN* CV6 .... 24 C1
Bathway Rd *COVS* CV3 .... 42 C5
Batsford Rd *COVN* CV6 .... 34 B2
Baulk La *RCOVN/BALC/EX* CV7 .... 38 D1
Bawnmore Ct
  RUGBYS/DCH CV22 .... 66 D4 ▯
Bawnmore Pk
  RUGBYS/DCH CV22 .... 67 E5
Bawnmore Rd
  RUGBYS/DCH CV22 .... 66 D4
Baxter Cl *TLHL/CAN* CV4 .... 33 E4
Bayley La *COV* CV1 .... 2 E4
Baylis Av *COVN* CV6 .... 16 A4
Bayton Rd *RCOVN/BALC/EX* CV7 .. 6 B5
  RCOVN/BALC/EX CV7 .... 16 C1
Bayton Wy *RCOVN/BALC/EX* CV7 .. 16 C1
Bay Tree Cl *COVE* CV2 .... 26 D2
Beacon Rd *COVN* CV6 .... 15 F5
Beaconsfield Av
  RUGBYS/DCH CV22 .... 67 G3
Beaconsfield Rd *COVE* CV2 .... 36 B4
Beake Av *COVN* CV6 .... 27 G3
Beamish Cl *COVE* CV2 .... 27 G5 ▯
Beanfield Av *COVS* CV3 .... 42 B5
Beatty Dr *RUGBYS/DCH* CV22 .... 66 D2
Beauchamp Rd *KNWTH* CV8 ...... 72 C5
Beaudesert Rd *COVW* CV5 .... 34 C5 ▯
Beaufort Dr *COVS* CV3 .... 45 F2
Beaumaris Cl *COVW* CV5 .... 32 D1
Beaumont Crs *COVN* CV6 .... 34 C2
Beaumont Rd
  RCOVN/BALC/EX CV7 .... 14 C2
  COVS CV3 .... 33 E3
Beausale Cft *COVW* CV5 .... 33 E3
Beckbury Rd *COVE* CV2 .... 27 F5 ▯
Beckfoot Dr *RUGBYN/HIL* CV21 .. 52 B1 ▯
Beckfoot Dr *COVE* CV2 .... 27 F2
Becks La *RCOVN/BALC/EX* CV7 ... 11 G3
Bede Rd *BDWTH* CV12 .... 6 A1
  COVN CV6 .... 34 D1
Bedford St *COV* CV1 .... 34 C4
Bedlam La *COVN* CV6 .... 25 G1
Bedworth Cl *BDWTH* CV12 .... 7 H3
Bedworth La *BDWTH* CV12 .... 5 E1
Bedworth Rd *BDWTH* CV12 .... 7 F3
  COVN CV6 .... 16 A3
Beechcroft *BDWTH* CV12 .... 5 H4 ▯
Beech Dr *KNWTH* CV8 .... 73 F2
  RRUGBY CV23 .... 74 D4 ▯
  RUGBYS/DCH CV22 .... 66 C3
The Beeches *BDWTH* CV12 .... 5 G3
Beechnut Cl *TLHL/CAN* CV4 ...... 32 B4
Beech Rd *COVN* CV6 .... 34 D1 ▯

Beech Tree Av *TLHL/CAN* CV4 .... 33 F4
Beechwood Av *COVW* CV5 .... 34 A5
Beechwood Cft *KNWTH* CV8 ..... 72 D5
Beechwood Rd *BDWTH* CV12 .... 6 C1
Beeston Cl *COVS* CV3 .... 45 F1
Beehive Hl *KNWTH* CV8 .... 56 B5
Belgrave Dr *RRUGBY* CV23 ...... 52 B3
Belgrave Rd *COVE* CV2 .... 36 D2
Belgrave Sq *COVE* CV2 .... 37 E2
Bellairs Av *BDWTH* CV12 .... 5 G4
Bellbrooke Cl *COVE* CV2 .... 26 B2
Bell Dr *RCOVN/BALC/EX* CV7 .... 15 G1
Bellemere Rd *HIA/OLT* B92 ...... 28 D1
Belle Vue Ter *HIA/OLT* B92 ...... 18 C5
Bell Green Rd *COVN* CV6 .... 26 A3
Bell Wk *RUGBYN/HIL* CV21 ...... 69 E4
Belmont Rd *COVN* CV6 .... 26 A4 ▯
  RUGBYS/DCH CV22 .... 67 G4
Belvedere Rd *COVW* CV5 .... 42 C1
Benedictine Ct *COVS* CV3 .... 43 E2
Bennetts Rd
  RCOVN/BALC/EX CV7 .... 14 B3
Bennetts Rd South
  RCOVN/BALC/EX CV7 .... 14 B5
Bennett St *RUGBYN/HIL* CV21 ... 67 F1 ▯
Bennfield Rd *RUGBYN/HIL* CV21 .. 67 G1
Benn Rd *BDWTH* CV12 .... 7 H3
Benn St *RUGBYS/DCH* CV22 ..... 68 A2
Benson Rd *COVN* CV6 .... 24 C2
Benthall Rd *COVN* CV6 .... 25 H1
Bentley Ct *COVN* CV6 .... 15 E4
Bentley Rd *RCOVN/BALC/EX* CV7 .. 6 A4
Benton Green La
  RCOVN/BALC/EX CV7 .... 31 F4
The Bentree *COVS* CV3 .... 44 B1
Beresford Av *COVN* CV6 .... 25 G2
Berkeley Rd *KNWTH* CV8 .... 72 C1
Berkeley Rd North *COVW* CV5 ... 34 C5
Berkeley Rd South *COVW* CV5 ... 42 C1
Berkett Rd *COVN* CV6 .... 14 D5
Berkswell Rd *COVN* CV6 .... 26 A1
Berners Cl *TLHL/CAN* CV4 .... 32 C4
Berry St *COV* CV1 .... 3 J3
Bertie Rd *KNWTH* CV8 .... 72 D3
Berwick Cl *COVW* CV5 .... 33 F2
Berwyn Av *COVN* CV6 .... 24 C2
Best Av *KNWTH* CV8 .... 57 G5
Beswick Gdns
  RUGBYS/DCH CV22 .... 66 D5
Bettman Cl *COVS* CV3 .... 43 G3
Beverley Cl *RCOVN/BALC/EX* CV7 .. 38 C2
Beverly Dr *TLHL/CAN* CV4 .... 57 H2
Bevington Crs *COVN* CV6 .... 34 A1
Bexfield Cl *COVW* CV5 .... 23 E5
Biart Pl *RUGBYN/HIL* CV21 ...... 68 B1
Bideford Rd *COVE* CV2 .... 26 C4
Bigbury Cl *COVS* CV3 .... 43 G4
Biggin Hall Crs *COVS* CV3 .... 36 B4
Biggin Hall La *RRUGBY* CV23 .... 74 B5
Bilberry Rd *COVE* CV2 .... 26 D1 ▯
Billesden Cl *COVS* CV3 .... 45 E1
Billing Rd *COVW* CV5 .... 33 H3
Billinton Cl *COVE* CV2 .... 37 E4
Bilton La *RRUGBY* CV23 .... 66 B2
Bilton Rd *RUGBYS/DCH* CV22 .... 66 D5
  RUGBYS/DCH CV22 .... 67 G2 ▯
Binley Av *COVS* CV3 .... 45 F2
Binley Gv *COVS* CV3 .... 45 F2 ▯
Binley Rd *COV* CV1 .... 3 K4
  COVE CV2 .... 36 B4
  COVS CV3 .... 36 A4
Binns Cl *TLHL/CAN* CV4 .... 40 D1
Binswood Cl *COVE* CV2 .... 26 D1
Binton Rd *COVE* CV2 .... 26 D1
Birch Cl *BDWTH* CV12 .... 6 D1
  COVW CV5 .... 32 D2 ▯
Birch Dr *RUGBYS/DCH* CV22 ..... 66 B2
Birches La *KNWTH* CV8 .... 73 E4
The Birches *BDWTH* CV12 .... 7 H1
Birchfield Rd *COVN* CV6 .... 24 B4
Birchgrave Cl *COVN* CV6 .... 26 A4 ▯
Birchwood Rd *COVS* CV3 .... 46 A2
Bird Grove Ct *COV* CV1 .... 35 F1
Bird St *COV* CV1 .... 2 E1
Birmingham Rd *COVW* CV5 ...... 22 D4
  KNWTH CV8 .... 55 H3
  KNWTH CV8 .... 58 D5
  RCOVN/BALC/EX CV7 .... 9 F5
  RCOVN/BALC/EX CV7 .... 20 A1
Birstall Dr *RRUGBY* CV23 .... 52 B3
Bishop St *COV* CV1 .... 2 D2
Bishops Wk *COVW* CV5 .... 42 D1
Bishopton Cl *COVW* CV5 .... 33 F3
Black Bank *RCOVN/BALC/EX* CV7 .. 6 B4
Blackberry Cl *RUGBYN/HIL* CV21 .. 52 B1
Blackberry La *COVN* CV6 .... 26 B5

RCOVN/BALC/EX CV7 .... 14 D3
Blackburn Rd *COVN* CV6 .... 15 H5
Blackfirs La
  CHWD/FDBR/MGN B37 .... 8 A1
Black Horse Rd
  RCOVN/BALC/EX CV7 .... 16 A2
Blackman Wy *RUGBYN/HIL* CV21 .. 51 F5
Black Prince Av *COVS* CV3 ...... 43 G3
Blackshaw Dr *COVE* CV2 .... 27 F5 ▯
Blackthorn Cl *TLHL/CAN* CV4 .... 41 H4
Blackthorne Rd *KNWTH* CV8 .... 73 E4
Blackwatch Rd *COVN* CV6 ...... 25 E3
Blackwell Rd *COVN* CV6 .... 25 G3 ▯
Blackwood Av
  RUGBYS/DCH CV22 .... 66 D2
Blair Dr *BDWTH* CV12 .... 5 E4
Blake Cl *RUGBYS/DCH* CV22 ..... 66 C2
Blandford Dr *COVE* CV2 .... 37 F1
Bleaberry *RUGBYN/HIL* CV21 .... 52 A2
Blenheim Av *COVN* CV6 .... 15 E5
Bletchley Dr *COVW* CV5 .... 33 F2
Blind La *RCOVN/BALC/EX* CV7 ... 30 D2
Blockley Rd *BDWTH* CV12 .... 6 C1
Blondvil St *COVS* CV3 .... 43 E2
Bloxam Gdns *RUGBYS/DCH* CV22 .. 67 F2
Bloxam Pl *RUGBYN/HIL* CV21 ... 67 G1 ▯
Bluebell Cl *RUGBYN/HIL* CV21 .. 52 B1 ▯
Bluebell Wk *TLHL/CAN* CV4 ..... 32 D5
The Blundells *KNWTH* CV8 ...... 72 D2
Blyth Av *RCOVN/BALC/EX* CV7 .. 38 C4
Blyth Cl *BDWTH* CV12 .... 5 E4
Blythe Rd *COV* CV1 .... 35 G2
Boar Cft *TLHL/CAN* CV4 .... 32 D4
Bockendon Rd *TLHL/CAN* CV4 ... 40 B5
Bodmin Rd *COVE* CV2 .... 37 F1
Bodnant Wy *KNWTH* CV8 .... 73 G1 ▯
Bohun St *TLHL/CAN* CV4 .... 32 D5
Bolingbroke Rd *COVS* CV3 .... 36 A5
Bolton Cl *COVS* CV3 .... 43 G4
Bond St *COV* CV1 .... 2 C3
  RUGBYN/HIL CV21 .... 67 F1
Bonington Dr *BDWTH* CV12 ...... 6 A1
Bonneville Cl *COVW* CV5 .... 21 H3
Bonnington Cl *RUGBYN/HIL* CV21 .. 69 F3
Borrowdale Rd *RUGBYN/HIL* CV21 .. 52 A1
Borrowdale Cl *COVN* CV6 .... 24 C2
Boston Pl *COVN* CV6 .... 25 F3
Boswell Dr *COVE* CV2 .... 27 G5 ▯
  COVE CV2 .... 27 G4 ▯
Boswell Rd *RUGBYS/DCH* CV22 .. 67 E5
Botoner Rd *COV* CV1 .... 3 J4
Bott Rd *COVW* CV5 .... 41 H1
Boughton Rd *RUGBYN/HIL* CV21 .. 52 A3
Boundary Rd *RUGBYN/HIL* CV21 .. 68 B3
Bourne Rd *COVS* CV3 .... 36 C5
Bowden Wy *COVS* CV3 .... 37 E5
Bow Fell *RUGBYN/HIL* CV21 ..... 52 B2
Bowfell Cl *COVW* CV5 .... 33 F2 ▯
Bowling Green La
  RCOVN/BALC/EX CV7 .... 15 G1
Bowls Ct *COVW* CV5 .... 34 B3
Bowness Cl *COVN* CV6 .... 24 C3
The Boxhill *COVS* CV3 .... 36 B5
Boyce Wy *RRUGBY* CV23 .... 50 B4
Boyd Cl *COVE* CV2 .... 27 F3
Bracadale Cl *COVS* CV3 .... 37 G4
Bracebridge Cl
  RCOVN/BALC/EX CV7 .... 38 B3 ▯
Bracken Cl *RUGBYS/DCH* CV22 .. 67 E3
Bracken Dr *RUGBYS/DCH* CV22 .. 67 E3
Brackenhurst Rd *COVN* CV6 ..... 24 B4
Brackley Cl *COVN* CV6 .... 24 B4
Braddock Cl *COVS* CV3 .... 37 G5
Brade Dr *COVE* CV2 .... 27 H5
Bradley Cft *RCOVN/BALC/EX* CV7 .. 38 B3
Bradney Gn *TLHL/CAN* CV4 ...... 40 C2
Bradnick Pl *TLHL/CAN* CV4 ...... 32 D5 ▯
Bradnock's Marsh La
  HIA/OLT B92 .... 29 G4
Braemar Cl *COVE* CV2 .... 27 E5
Bramble St *COV* CV1 .... 3 H4
Brampton Wy *BDWTH* CV12 ..... 7 H2 ▯
Bramston Crs *TLHL/CAN* CV4 .... 32 D5
Bramwell Gdns *COVN* CV6 ...... 15 H3 ▯
Brandfield Rd *COVN* CV6 .... 24 B3 ▯
Brandon La *KNWTH* CV8 .... 44 D5
  KNWTH CV8 .... 46 D4
Brandon Rd *COVS* CV3 .... 45 G1
  KNWTH CV8 .... 47 G3
Branksome Rd *COVN* CV6 ...... 24 A5
Bransdale Av *COVN* CV6 .... 15 F5
Bransford Av *TLHL/CAN* CV4 .... 41 H4
Branstree Dr *COVN* CV6 .... 25 F1
Brathay Cl *COVS* CV3 .... 43 F3
Braunston Pl *RUGBYS/DCH* CV22 .. 68 A4
Brayford Av *COVS* CV3 .... 43 E3
Bray's La *COVE* CV2 .... 36 A3
Braytoft Cl *COVN* CV6 .... 25 E1 ▯

Brazil St *TLHL/CAN* CV4 .... 32 C [?]
Bredon Av *COVS* CV3 .... 45 F2
Bree Cl *COVW* CV5 .... 23 E [?]
Bree's La *KNWTH* CV8 .... 54 A [?]
Brentwood Av *COVS* CV3 .... 59 E [?]
Bretford Rd *COVE* CV2 .... 26 C [?]
Bretts Cl *COV* CV1 .... 35 C [?]
Brewers Cl *COVS* CV3 .... 37 C [?]
Brewster Cl *COVE* CV2 .... 37 E [?]
Briansway *COVN* CV6 .... 15 C [?]
Briardene Av *BDWTH* CV12 ...... 6 E [?]
Briars Cl *COVE* CV2 .... 36 C [?]
  RRUGBY CV23 .... 50 B [?]
Brick Hill La *COVW* CV5 .... 22 B [?]
The Bridal Pth *COVW* CV5 ...... 23 F [?]
Bridgeacre Gdns *COVS* CV3 ..... 37 F [?]
Bridgecote *COVS* CV3 .... 45 E [?]
Bridgeman Rd *COVN* CV6 .... 34 D [?]
Bridge St *COVN* CV6 .... 26 A4 ▯
  RUGBYN/HIL CV21 .... 68 A [?]
Bridget St *RUGBYN/HIL* CV21 ... 67 F [?]
Bridle Brook La
  RCOVN/BALC/EX CV7 .... 13 E [?]
Bridle Rd *RUGBYN/HIL* CV21 .... 51 E [?]
Bridport Cl *COVE* CV2 .... 37 G [?]
Brierley Rd *COVE* CV2 .... 26 C3 ▯
Brightmere Rd *COVN* CV6 ...... 34 D [?]
Brighton St *COVE* CV2 .... 3 K [?]
Bright St *COVN* CV6 .... 25 G [?]
Brightwalton Rd *COVS* CV3 ..... 43 F [?]
Brill Cl *TLHL/CAN* CV4 .... 41 G [?]
Brindle Av *COVS* CV3 .... 36 C [?]
Brindley Paddocks *COV* CV1 .... 2 C [?]
  COV CV1 .... 35 E [?]
Brindley Rd *RCOVN/BALC/EX* CV7 .. 16 B [?]
  RUGBYN/HIL CV21 .... 69 E [?]
Brinklow Rd *COVS* CV3 .... 37 G [?]
Brisbane Cl *COVS* CV3 .... 43 G3 ▯
Briscoe Rd *COVN* CV6 .... 15 E [?]
Bristol Rd *COVW* CV5 .... 34 B [?]
Britannia St *COVE* CV2 .... 3 J [?]
Briton Rd *COVE* CV2 .... 36 A [?]
Brixham Dr *COVE* CV2 .... 26 C [?]
Brixworth Cl *COVS* CV3 .... 45 E [?]
Broadgate *COV* CV1 .... 2 D [?]
Broadlands Cl *TLHL/CAN* CV4 ... 33 G [?]
Broad La *RCOVN/BALC/EX* CV7 .. 31 C [?]
  TLHL/CAN CV4 .... 33 G [?]
Broadmere Ri *TLHL/CAN* CV4 ... 33 E [?]
Broad Park Rd *COVE* CV2 ...... 26 D [?]
Broad St *COVN* CV6 .... 26 A [?]
Broad Street Jetty *COVN* CV6 .. 25 G4 ▯
Broadwater *COVW* CV5 .... 42 C [?]
Broadway *COVW* CV5 .... 34 C [?]
Broadwell Ct *TLHL/CAN* CV4 .... 40 D [?]
Broadwells Crs *TLHL/CAN* CV4 .. 40 D [?]
Brockenhurst Wy *COVN* CV6 .... 16 B2 ▯
Brockhurst Dr *TLHL/CAN* CV4 ... 32 B4 ▯
Bromleigh Dr *COVE* CV2 .... 36 C [?]
Bromley Cl *KNWTH* CV8 .... 72 C [?]
Bromwich Cl *COVS* CV3 .... 45 F2 ▯
Bromwich Rd *RUGBYN/HIL* CV21 .. 68 D [?]
Bronte Cl *RUGBYN/HIL* CV21 .... 68 B [?]
Brook Cl *COV* CV1 .... 3 H [?]
Brooke Rd *KNWTH* CV8 .... 73 F [?]
Brookford Av *COVN* CV6 .... 14 C [?]
Brook Green La *HIA/OLT* B92 ... 28 C [?]
Brooklea *BDWTH* CV12 .... 5 H3 ▯
Brooklime Dr *RUGBYN/HIL* CV21 .. 52 C [?]
Brooklyn Rd *COVN* CV6 .... 25 F [?]
Brookshaw Wy *COVE* CV2 ...... 27 F [?]
Brookside Av *COVW* CV5 .... 33 G [?]
  KNWTH CV8 .... 72 C [?]
Brookside Cl *RUGBYS/DCH* CV22 .. 67 G [?]
Brook St *KNWTH* CV8 .... 63 E [?]
Brookvale Av *COVS* CV3 .... 37 E [?]
Brook Vw *RUGBYS/DCH* CV22 .. 67 E3 ▯
Broom Cl *RUGBYS/DCH* CV22 ... 67 E3 ▯
Broome Cft *COVN* CV6 .... 14 D [?]
Broomfield Pl *COVW* CV5 ...... 34 C [?]
Broomfield Rd *COVW* CV5 ...... 34 B [?]
Broomybank *KNWTH* CV8 ...... 73 F [?]
Browett Rd *COVN* CV6 .... 34 B [?]
Browning Rd *COVE* CV2 .... 36 C [?]
  RUGBYN/HIL CV21 .... 69 F [?]
Brownshill Ct *COVN* CV6 .... 24 B [?]
Brownshill Green Rd *COVN* CV6 .. 24 B [?]
  COVW CV5 .... 24 A [?]
Brown's La *COVW* CV5 .... 23 F [?]
Brownsover La
  RUGBYN/HIL CV21 .... 51 H2 [?]
Brownsover Rd
  RUGBYN/HIL CV21 .... 51 E [?]
Bruce Rd *COVN* CV6 .... 24 C [?]
  RCOVN/BALC/EX CV7 .... 15 H [?]
Bruce Williams Wy
  RUGBYS/DCH CV22 .... 67 H [?]
Brunel Cl *COVE* CV2 .... 3 J3

Brunswick Cl
  RUGBYN/HIL CV21 .... 52 A3 🔟
Brunswick Rd *COV* CV1 .... 2 A5 🔟
  COV CV1 .... 34 C4
Bruntingthorpe Wy *COVS* CV3 ... 45 E1
Brunton Cl *COVS* CV3 .... 37 H5 🔟
Bryanston Cl *COVE* CV2 .... 37 G2 🔟
Bryant Rd *RCOVN/BALC/EX* CV7 .. 16 A1
Brympton Rd *COVS* CV3 .... 36 C4
Bryn Jones Cl *COVS* CV3 .... 45 F2
Bryn Rd *COVN* CV6 .... 25 H4
Buccleuch Cl
  RUGBYS/DCH CV22 .... 75 G3 🔟
Buchanan Rd *RUGBYS/DCH* CV22 .. 67 E3
Buckfast Cl *COVS* CV3 .... 43 G4
Buckhold Dr *COVW* CV5 .... 33 F1
Buckingham Ri *COVW* CV5 .... 33 F2
Buckland Rd *COVN* CV6 .... 24 D1 🔟
Bucknill Crs *RUGBYN/HIL* CV21 .. 69 F4
Buckwell La *RRUGBY* CV23 .... 53 F3
Budbrooke Cl *COVE* CV2 .... 26 D1
Bulkington Rd *BDWTH* CV12 .... 6 D3 🔟
Bullfield Av *TLHL/CAN* CV4 .... 32 C5
Bullimore Gv *KNWTH* CV8 .... 73 E5
Bull's Head La *COVS* CV3 .... 36 A5
Bull Yd *COV* CV1 .... 2 C4
Bulwer Rd *COVN* CV6 .... 24 C4
Bulwick Cl *COVS* CV3 .... 37 H5 🔟
Burbages La *COVN* CV6 .... 15 F3
Burberry Gv
  RCOVN/BALC/EX CV7 .... 38 A3
Burbury Cl *BDWTH* CV12 .... 6 C1 🔟
Burges *COV* CV1 .... 2 D2
Burleigh Cl *RCOVN/BALC/EX* CV7 .. 38 B2
Burlington Rd *COVE* CV2 .... 35 H2
Burnaby Rd *COVN* CV6 .... 25 E3
Burnham Rd *COVS* CV3 .... 44 A3
Burnsall Gv *COVW* CV5 .... 41 H1
Burnsall Rd *COVW* CV5 .... 41 H1
Burnside *COVS* CV3 .... 37 G4
  RUGBYS/DCH CV22 .... 67 E2
Burns Rd *COVE* CV2 .... 36 B3
Burns Wk *BDWTH* CV12 .... 6 C4
Burrow Hill La
  RCOVN/BALC/EX CV7 .... 13 H1
Burton Cl *COVW* CV5 .... 23 C2
Busby Cl *COVS* CV3 .... 45 F2
Bushbery Av *TLHL/CAN* CV4 .... 32 D5
Bush Cl *TLHL/CAN* CV4 .... 32 D3
Butcher's La *COVW* CV5 .... 23 G5
Butchers Rd *HIA/OLT* B92 .... 18 C5 🔟
Butler Cl *KNWTH* CV8 .... 57 G5 🔟
Butlers Crs *RCOVN/BALC/EX* CV7 .. 6 A4
Butlers End *RWWCK/WEL* CV35 ..... 70 C5
Butlers Leap *RUGBYN/HIL* CV21 .. 52 B4
Butlin Rd *COVN* CV6 .... 15 E4
  RUGBYN/HIL CV21 .... 68 B1
Buttermere *RUGBYN/HIL* CV21 .. 52 B3
Buttermere Cl *COVS* CV3 .... 45 F2 🔟
Butterworth Dr *TLHL/CAN* CV4 .. 41 E3
Butt La *COVW* CV5 .... 23 F4
Butts *COV* CV1 .... 2 A5
Butts Rd *COV* CV1 .... 2 A4
Byfield Rd *COVN* CV6 .... 34 A1
Byron Av *BDWTH* CV12 .... 6 D3 🔟
Byron St *COV* CV1 .... 2 E1
Bywater Cl *COVS* CV3 .... 42 D4

C

Cadden Dr *TLHL/CAN* CV4 .... 33 F4
Cadman Cl *BDWTH* CV12 .... 6 C2 🔟
Caesar Rd *KNWTH* CV8 .... 72 C4
Caithness Cl *COVW* CV5 .... 33 E2
Caldecote Rd *COVN* CV6 .... 35 E1
Caldecott Pl *RUGBYN/HIL* CV21 .. 68 A2
Caldecott St *RUGBYN/HIL* CV21... 68 A2
Calder Cl *BDWTH* CV12 .... 7 H3
  COVS CV3 .... 43 G2
Calmere Cl *COVE* CV2 .... 27 F3
Caludon Park Av *COVE* CV2 .... 37 E1
Caludon Rd *COVE* CV2 .... 36 A2
Calvert Cl *COVS* CV3 .... 43 F3
Cambridge St *COV* CV1 .... 35 G1
  RUGBYN/HIL CV21 .... 68 A1
Camden St *COVE* CV2 .... 36 A2
Cameron Cl *COVW* CV5 .... 23 E4
Campbell St *RUGBYN/HIL* CV21 .. 67 E1
Campion Cl *COVS* CV3 .... 43 F3
Campion Wy *RUGBYN/HIL* CV21 .. 52 B1
Campling Cl *BDWTH* CV12 .... 7 H3 🔟
Camville *COVS* CV3 .... 37 G4
Canal Rd *COVN* CV6 .... 25 G3
Canberra Rd *COVE* CV2 .... 16 C4
Canford Cl *COVS* CV3 .... 59 E1
Canley Ford *COVW* CV5 .... 42 A2

Canley Rd *COVW* CV5 .... 34 A5
  COVW CV5 .... 41 H1
Cannocks La *TLHL/CAN* CV4 .... 41 H5
Cannon Cl *TLHL/CAN* CV4 .... 42 A3
Cannon Hill Rd *TLHL/CAN* CV4 ... 41 H5
Cannon Park Rd *TLHL/CAN* CV4 .. 42 A4
Canon Dr *RCOVN/BALC/EX* CV7 ... 15 F2
Canon Hudson Cl *COVS* CV3 ..... 44 C3 🔟
Canterbury St *COV* CV1 .... 3 G1
Cantlow Cl *COVW* CV5 .... 33 E3
Capmartin Rd *COVN* CV6 .... 24 D4
Capulet Cl *COVS* CV3 .... 44 C3
Caradoc Cl *COVE* CV2 .... 26 D4
Cardale Cft *COVS* CV3 .... 45 F1
Cardigan Rd *BDWTH* CV12 .... 5 E4
Carding Cl *COVW* CV5 .... 32 D2
Carey St *COVN* CV6 .... 26 B2
Cargill Cl *COVN* CV6 .... 15 H3
Carlton Cl *BDWTH* CV12 .... 7 H2 🔟
Carlton Rd *COVN* CV6 .... 35 E1
  RUGBYS/DCH CV22 .... 66 D3
Carmelite Rd *COV* CV1 .... 3 H4
Carnbroe Av *COVS* CV3 .... 45 E3
Carnegie Cl *COVS* CV3 .... 44 B3
Carsal Cl *RCOVN/BALC/EX* CV7 ... 15 F3
Carter Rd *COVS* CV3 .... 44 A1
Carthusian Rd *COVS* CV3 .... 43 E1
Cartmel Cl *COVW* CV5 .... 33 E2 🔟
Carvell Cl *COVE* CV2 .... 23 F2
Carver Cl *COVE* CV2 .... 37 E4
Cascade Cl *COVS* CV3 .... 43 G3
Cashmore Rd *BDWTH* CV12 .... 5 G4
  KNWTH CV8 .... 73 G3
Cash's La *COV* CV1 .... 25 F5
Casia Gv *KNWTH* CV8 .... 73 G3
Caspian Wy *COVE* CV2 .... 27 G3 🔟
Cassandra Cl *TLHL/CAN* CV4 ...... 57 H1
Castle Cl *COVS* CV3 .... 43 F3
Castle Hl *KNWTH* CV8 .... 72 C2
Castle Ms *RUGBYN/HIL* CV21 .... 67 H1 🔟
Castle Rd *KNWTH* CV8 .... 72 C3
Castle St *COV* CV1 .... 3 G1
  RUGBYN/HIL CV21 .... 67 H1 🔟
Catesby Rd *COVN* CV6 .... 24 D3
  RUGBYS/DCH CV22 .... 68 B3
Catherine St *COV* CV1 .... 3 J2
Cavans Wy *COVS* CV3 .... 45 G1
Cavendish Rd *TLHL/CAN* CV4 ...... 41 H3
Cawnpore Rd *COVN* CV6 .... 24 D1
Cawston La *RUGBYS/DCH* CV22 .. 66 A5
Cawston Wy
  RUGBYS/DCH CV22 .... 66 C4 🔟
Cawthorne Cl *COV* CV1 .... 35 G2 🔟
Cecily Rd *COVS* CV3 .... 43 F2
Cedars Av *COVN* CV6 .... 34 A1
Cedars Rd *RCOVN/BALC/EX* CV7 .. 6 B4
Cedar Wood Dr
  RCOVN/BALC/EX CV7 .... 38 B3
Cedric Cl *COVS* CV3 .... 44 C4
Celandine *RUGBYN/HIL* CV21 .... 52 B1
Celandine Rd *COVE* CV2 .... 26 D1 🔟
Centaur Rd *COVW* CV5 .... 34 B4
Centenary Rd *TLHL/CAN* CV4 ...... 41 H2
Centenary Wy *KNWTH* CV8 .... 57 E3
  KNWTH CV8 .... 57 E3
  KNWTH CV8 .... 73 H1
Central Av *COVE* CV2 .... 36 A4
Chace Av *COVS* CV3 .... 44 B4
Chaceley Cl *COVE* CV2 .... 27 G3
Chadwick Cl *COVW* CV5 .... 33 F3
Chalfont Cl *BDWTH* CV12 .... 6 A1
  COVW CV5 .... 33 F2
Challenge Cl *COV* CV1 .... 35 F2
Chamberlaine St *BDWTH* CV12 ..... 6 B1
Chamberlain Rd
  RUGBYN/HIL CV21 .... 69 F4
Chancellors Cl *TLHL/CAN* CV4 .... 41 H5
Chandos St *COVE* CV2 .... 36 A3
The Chantries *COV* CV1............ 35 G1
Chapel Dr *RCOVN/BALC/EX* CV7 .. 38 B1
Chapel Farm Cl *COVS* CV3 ..... 44 C3 🔟
Chapel La *KNWTH* CV8 .... 61 G2
  RCOVN/BALC/EX CV7 .... 17 H2
Chapel St *BDWTH* CV12............ 6 B1
  COV CV1 .... 2 C2 🔟
  RRUGBY CV23 .... 50 A5
  RUGBYN/HIL CV21 .... 67 G1
Chard Rd *COVS* CV3 .... 44 D1
Charity Rd *RCOVN/BALC/EX* CV7 .. 14 B1
Charlecote Rd *COVN* CV6 .... 24 C1
Charles Eaton Rd *BDWTH* CV12 .. 5 H2
Charlesfield Rd
  RUGBYS/DCH CV22 .... 67 G4
Charles St *COV* CV1 .... 3 G1
  RUGBYS/DCH CV22 .... 67 F2
Charles Warren Cl
  RUGBYN/HIL CV21 .... 67 H1
Charlewood Rd *COVN* CV6............ 24 D1

Charlotte St *RUGBYN/HIL* CV21.... 67 H1
Charminster Dr *COVS* CV3 .... 43 F5
Charter Av *TLHL/CAN* CV4 .... 40 B2
Charterhouse Rd *COV* CV1............ 3 H4
Charter Rd *RUGBYS/DCH* CV22 .... 68 C4
Charwelton Dr *RRUGBY* CV23 ...... 52 C3
Chase La *KNWTH* CV8 .... 71 F1
Chatham Cl *COVS* CV3 .... 44 C1 🔟
Chatsworth Gv *KNWTH* CV8 ..... 73 G2 🔟
Chatsworth Ri *COVS* CV3 .... 43 G4
Chattaway Dr
  RCOVN/BALC/EX CV7 .... 38 B3
Chauntry Pl *COV* CV1 .... 2 E2
Cheadle Cl *COVE* CV2 .... 16 A4
Cheam Cl *COVN* CV6 .... 26 A2
Chelney Wk *COVS* CV3 .... 37 G5
Chelsey Rd *COVE* CV2 .... 27 E3
Cheltenham Cl *BDWTH* CV12 .... 6 B1 🔟
Cheltenham Cft *COVE* CV2 ...... 27 F4 🔟
Chelveston Rd *COVN* CV6............ 34 A1
Chelwood Gv *COVE* CV2 .... 27 F2 🔟
Chenies Cl *COVW* CV5 .... 33 F3
Chepstow Cl *COVS* CV3 .... 44 C4
Cheriton Cl *COVW* CV5 .... 33 H2
Cherrybrook Wy *COVE* CV2 .... 26 C2
Cherry Cl *COVN* CV6 .... 25 F1
Cherry Gv *RUGBYS/DCH* CV22 .... 67 E2
Cherry Orch *KNWTH* CV8 .... 73 E2
Cherry Wy *KNWTH* CV8 .... 73 E2
Cherrywood Gv *COVW* CV5 ...... 32 D1
Cherwell Wy *RRUGBY* CV23 ..... 50 B5 🔟
Chesford Crs *COVN* CV6 .... 26 B1
Cheshire Cl *RUGBYS/DCH* CV22 .. 66 C4 🔟
Chesholme Rd *COVN* CV6............ 14 D5
The Chesils *COVS* CV3 .... 43 E4
Chester Rd *RCOVN/BALC/EX* CV7 .... 8 D4
Chester St *COV* CV1 .... 2 A2
  RUGBYN/HIL CV21 .... 52 A5 🔟
Chesterton Rd *COVN* CV6 .... 24 C3
Chestnut Av *KNWTH* CV8 .... 72 D4
Chestnut Fld *RUGBYN/HIL* CV21 .. 67 G1
Chestnut Gv *KNWTH* CV8 .... 63 E1 🔟
  TLHL/CAN CV4 .... 33 E4 🔟
Chestnut Rd *BDWTH* CV12 .... 5 G1
The Chestnuts *BDWTH* CV12 ..... 5 G3 🔟
Chestnut Tree Av *TLHL/CAN* CV4... 33 E4
Cheswick Cl *COVN* CV6 .... 26 A4 🔟
Chetwode Cl *COVW* CV5 .... 33 F2
Cheveral Av *COVN* CV6 .... 24 D5
  COVN CV6 .... 34 D1
Cheveral Rd *BDWTH* CV12 .... 6 A2
Cheylesmore *COV* CV1 .... 2 D5
Chicory Dr *RUGBYN/HIL* CV21 .... 52 B1
Chideock Hl *COVS* CV3 .... 42 C3
Chiel Cl *COVW* CV5 .... 32 D2
Childs Oak Cl
  RCOVN/BALC/EX CV7 .... 38 A3
Chillaton Rd *COVN* CV6 .... 24 D1
Chiltern Leys *COVN* CV6 .... 34 C2 🔟
The Chilterns *COVW* CV5 .... 33 F2 🔟
Chingford Rd *COVN* CV6............ 16 A4
Christchurch Rd *COVN* CV6 .... 24 B5
Church Cl *KNWTH* CV8 .... 61 H2 🔟
Churchill Av *COVN* CV6 .... 25 G2
  KNWTH CV8 .... 73 E1 🔟
Churchill Rd *RUGBYS/DCH* CV22 .. 67 G3
Church La *COVE* CV2 .... 36 B3
  COVW CV5 .... 32 A1
  RCOVN/BALC/EX CV7 .... 13 F1
  RCOVN/BALC/EX CV7 .... 15 G1
  RCOVN/BALC/EX CV7 .... 21 E3
  RCOVN/BALC/EX CV7 .... 30 C3
  RRUGBY CV23 .... 74 D5
Church Park Cl *COVN* CV6 ...... 24 B2 🔟
Church Rd *KNWTH* CV8 .... 59 H2
  KNWTH CV8 .... 61 H2
  RRUGBY CV23 .... 49 E4
Church St *COV* CV1 .... 35 F2
  RRUGBY CV23 .... 53 E4
  RUGBYN/HIL CV21 .... 67 G1
Church Wk *COVW* CV5 .... 23 G5
  RRUGBY CV23 .... 74 D4
  RUGBYN/HIL CV21 .... 67 H1
  RUGBYS/DCH CV22 .... 66 D4
Church Wy *BDWTH* CV12 .... 6 B2
Chylds Ct *COVW* CV5 .... 33 E1
Clara St *COVE* CV2 .... 36 A4
Clare Ct *RUGBYN/HIL* CV21...... 67 F1
Claremont Cl *BDWTH* CV12 .... 7 H1
Claremont Rd *RUGBYN/HIL* CV21 .. 68 A1
Claremont Wk *COVW* CV5 .... 23 G5
Clarence Rd *RUGBYN/HIL* CV21 .. 67 E1
Clarence St *COV* CV1 .... 3 H1
Clarendon Rd *KNWTH* CV8 ..... 73 E4 🔟
Clarendon St *COVW* CV5 .... 34 B5
Clarke's Av *KNWTH* CV8 .... 73 E4
Clark St *COVN* CV6 .... 26 A2
Claverdon Cl *COVS* CV3 .... 33 F3

Clayhill La *RRUGBY* CV23 .... 49 H4
Clay La *COVE* CV2 .... 36 A2
  COVW CV5 .... 12 C4
Clayton Rd *COVN* CV6 .... 34 A1
Clements St *COVE* CV2 .... 36 A3
Clennon Ri *COVE* CV2 .... 26 D3
Cleveland Rd *BDWTH* CV12 .... 7 H2
  COVE CV2 .... 36 A2
Clifden Gv *KNWTH* CV8 .... 73 G1
Clifford Bridge Rd *COVE* CV2 ..... 27 F5
  COVE CV2 .... 37 F2
  COVS CV3 .... 37 F4
Clifton Rd *RUGBYN/HIL* CV21...... 67 H1
Clifton St *COV* CV1 .... 35 G2
Clinton Av *KNWTH* CV8 .... 72 B1
Clinton La *KNWTH* CV8 .... 72 B1
Clinton Rd *COVN* CV6 .... 25 H1
Clipstone Rd *COVN* CV6 .... 24 A5
Clive Rd *RCOVN/BALC/EX* CV7 .... 38 C4
Cloister Cft *COVE* CV2 .... 27 F5
The Close *KNWTH* CV8 .... 46 D4
Cloud Gn *TLHL/CAN* CV4 .... 41 H4
Clovelly Gdns *COVE* CV2 ...... 36 C1 🔟
Clovelly Rd *COVE* CV2 .... 36 B1
Clover Cl *RUGBYN/HIL* CV21 .... 52 B1
Clyde Rd *BDWTH* CV12 .... 7 G2
Coalpit Fields Rd *BDWTH* CV12... 6 C3
Coalpit La *KNWTH* CV8 .... 47 G5
  KNWTH CV8 .... 63 H2
Coat of Arms Bridge Rd
  COVS CV3 .... 42 C3
Cobbs Rd *KNWTH* CV8 .... 72 B1
Cobden St *COVN* CV6 .... 35 G1
Cockerill's Meadow
  RUGBYN/HIL CV21 .... 69 E4
Colebrook Cl *COVS* CV3 .... 37 F4
Coleby Cl *TLHL/CAN* CV4 .... 40 B3
Coleman St *TLHL/CAN* CV4 .... 32 D3
Coleridge Rd *COVE* CV2 .... 36 C2
Colina Cl *COVS* CV3 .... 44 C4
Colledge Rd *COVN* CV6 .... 25 F2
Collett Wk *COV* CV1............ 2 A1
Colliery La *RCOVN/BALC/EX* CV7 .. 6 B4
Collingwood Av
  RUGBYS/DCH CV22 .... 66 C3
Collingwood Rd *COVW* CV5 ...... 34 C4
Collins Gv *TLHL/CAN* CV4 .... 41 H4
Columbia Gdns *BDWTH* CV12 ..... 6 D3
Colyere Cl *RCOVN/BALC/EX* CV7 .. 14 C2
Common La *KNWTH* CV8 .... 57 F5
  RCOVN/BALC/EX CV7 .... 12 C1
Common Wy *COVE* CV2 .... 36 C1
Compton Rd *COVN* CV6 .... 25 F1
Comrie Cl *COVE* CV2 .... 27 F5
Congleton Cl *COVN* CV6 .... 25 G1
Conifer Cl *BDWTH* CV12 .... 6 C1
Conifer Paddock *COVS* CV3 ...... 37 E5
Coniston Cl *RUGBYN/HIL* CV21 .. 52 B3
Coniston Dr *COVW* CV5 .... 32 B2 🔟
Coniston Rd *COVW* CV5 .... 34 B5
Conrad Rd *COVN* CV6 .... 24 C4
Constable Rd *RUGBYN/HIL* CV21.. 69 F3
Constance Cl *RCOVN/BALC/EX* CV7.. 5 H5
Consul Rd *RUGBYN/HIL* CV21...... 51 G3
Convent Cl *KNWTH* CV8 .... 57 E5
Conway Av *TLHL/CAN* CV4 .... 40 B1
Cook Cl *RUGBYN/HIL* CV21 ...... 52 A2
Cooke Cl *COVN* CV6 .... 16 A3
Cook St *COV* CV1 .... 2 D2
Coombe Ct *COVS* CV3 .... 37 G4
Coombe Dr *COVS* CV3 .... 46 C2 🔟
Coombe Park Rd *COVS* CV3 ...... 37 F4
Coombe St *COVS* CV3 .... 36 B4
Co-operative St *COVN* CV6 ...... 16 B5
Cope Arnolds Cl *COVN* CV6 ...... 15 H4 🔟
Copeland *RUGBYN/HIL* CV21 ..... 52 A2
Cope St *COV* CV1 .... 3 F3
Copland Pl *TLHL/CAN* CV4 ...... 32 C5 🔟
Coplow Cl *RCOVN/BALC/EX* CV7 .. 38 A3
Copperas St *COVE* CV2 .... 26 B1 🔟
Copper Beech Cl *COVN* CV6 ..... 25 G2
Copperfield Rd *COVE* CV2 .... 36 B3
The Coppice *COVS* CV3 .... 44 B1
Copse Cl *COVW* CV5 .... 21 H3
The Copse *RCOVN/BALC/EX* CV7 .. 6 A5
Copsewood Ter *COVS* CV3 ...... 36 C4
Copthorne Rd *COVN* CV6 .... 24 B3
Copt Oak Cl *TLHL/CAN* CV4....... 40 A2
Coral Cl *COVW* CV5............ 33 G4
Corbetts Cl *HIA/OLT* B92 .... 18 D4
Corbett St *RUGBYN/HIL* CV21 .. 52 A5
Corfe Cl *COVE* CV2 .... 37 F1
Corley Vw
  RCOVN/BALC/EX CV7 .... 15 E1 🔟
Cornelius St *COVS* CV3 .... 43 F1
Cornets End La
  RCOVN/BALC/EX CV7 .... 19 G4
The Cornfield *COVS* CV3 .... 36 C5

Cornflower Dr *RUGBYN/HIL* CV21.. **52** A1
Cornhill Gv *KNWTH* CV8 .... **73** G2
Cornwallis Rd *RUGBYS/DCH* CV22.. **66** B3
Cornwall Rd *COV* CV1 .... **3** G6
Coronation Rd *COV* CV1 ....
  RRUGBY CV23 .... **48** D4
Coronel Av *COVN* CV6 .... **15** G4
Corporation St *COV* CV1................ **2** C3
  RUGBYN/HIL CV21 .... **67** G1
Cotman Cl *BDWTH* CV12 .... **6** A1 ▣
Coton Rd *RUGBYN/HIL* CV21...... **69** E4
Cotswold Dr *COVS* CV3 .... **59** E1
Cottage Farm Rd *COVN* CV6 ...... **24** C2
Cottage Leap *RUGBYN/HIL* CV21... **52** B5
Cotterell Rd *RUGBYN/HIL* CV21.... **51** F3
Cottesbrook Cl *COVS* CV3 .... **37** E5
Cotton Dr *KNWTH* CV8 .... **73** G1 ▣
Coundon Gn *COVN* CV6................ **24** A3
Coundon Rd *COV* CV1 .... **2** A2
Coundon St *COV* CV1 .... **2** A2
Coundon Wedge Dr *COVW* CV5... **23** G5
The Countess's Cft *COVS* CV3 ... **43** F2 ▣
Courtaulds Wy *COVN* CV6 .... **25** F5
Courthouse Cft *KNWTH* CV8 ...... **73** G3
Courtland Av *COVN* CV6 .... **34** B1
Court Leet *COVS* CV3 .... **46** B2
Court Leet Rd *COVS* CV3.............. **43** G2
Coventry Rd *BDWTH* CV12 .... **6** B4
  HIA/OLT B92 .... **8** D5
  KNWTH CV8 .... **59** E5
  KNWTH CV8 .... **73** E1
  RCOVN/BALC/EX CV7 .... **17** E3
  RCOVN/BALC/EX CV7 .... **30** D3
  RRUGBY CV23 .... **48** B4
  RRUGBY CV23 .... **74** B3
  RUGBYS/DCH CV22 .... **66** B3
  RUGBYS/DCH CV22 .... **74** D1
Coventry Road Exhall
  RCOVN/BALC/EX CV7 .... **16** A1
Coventry St *COV* CV2 .... **36** A2
Coventry Wy *BDWTH* CV12 .... **5** F3
  KNWTH CV8 .... **62** D1
  RCOVN/BALC/EX CV7 .... **11** H2
  RCOVN/BALC/EX CV7 .... **31** E2
Cove Pl *COVE* CV2 .... **26** C4
Coverley Pl *RUGBYS/DCH* CV22.. **67** E1
Cowan Cl *RUGBYS/DCH* CV22...... **66** B3
Cowley Rd *COVE* CV2 .... **36** D2
Cox Crs *RUGBYS/DCH* CV22 .... **75** G3
Cox St *COV* CV1 .... **3** F2
Cozens Cl *BDWTH* CV12 .... **6** A1
Crabmill La *COVN* CV6................... **25** H4
Crackley La *KNWTH* CV8 .... **40** C5
Craigends Av *COVS* CV3 .... **45** E3
Crakston Cl *COVE* CV2 .... **37** E4
Cramper's Fld *COVN* CV6 .... **34** C1
Cranborne Cha *COVE* CV2 .... **37** F1
Craner's Rd *COVE* CV2 .... **35** H2
Cranford Rd *COVW* CV5 .... **33** H2
Crathie Cl *COVE* CV2 .... **37** F5
Craven Av *COVS* CV3 .... **46** A2
Craven Rd *RUGBYN/HIL* CV21 ..... **51** F5
Craven St *COVW* CV5 .... **34** B4
Crecy Rd *COVS* CV3 .... **43** G2
Crescent Av *COVS* CV3 .... **36** B4
The Crescent *HIA/OLT* B92 .... **18** D4
  RCOVN/BALC/EX CV7 .... **14** B2
  RRUGBY CV23 .... **74** A1
Cressage Rd *COVE* CV2 .... **27** G5
Crew La *KNWTH* CV8 .... **73** H1
Cricket La *COVW* CV5 .... **34** B3
Crick Rd *RUGBYN/HIL* CV21 .... **69** G5
Critchley Dr *RUGBYS/DCH* CV22.. **75** H4
Croft Flds *BDWTH* CV12 .... **6** B3
Croft Pool *BDWTH* CV12 .... **5** H3
Croft Rd *BDWTH* CV12 .... **5** H3
  COV CV1 .... **2** B4
The Croft *BDWTH* CV12 .... **7** H3
  COVN CV6................................ **15** H4
  RCOVN/BALC/EX CV7 .... **20** C2
Cromarty Cl *COVW* CV5 .... **33** E1 ▣
Cromes Wd *TLHL/CAN* CV4 .... **32** B5
Cromwell La *TLHL/CAN* CV4 .... **40** A3
Cromwell Rd *RUGBYS/DCH* CV22 .. **68** A3
Cromwell St *COVN* CV6 .... **25** H5
Crondal Rd *RCOVN/BALC/EX* CV7.. **16** B1
Croome Cl *COVN* CV6 .... **34** B2 ▣
Crosbie Rd *COVW* CV5 .... **34** A3
Cross Cheaping *COV* CV1 .... **2** D3 ▣
Cross Rd *COVN* CV6 .... **25** H3
  RCOVN/BALC/EX CV7 .... **14** B2 ▣
Cross St *COV* CV1 .... **3** F1
  RRUGBY CV23 .... **50** A4
  RUGBYS/DCH CV22 .... **52** A5
Crossway Rd *COVS* CV3 .... **42** D5
Crowmere Rd *COVE* CV2 .... **27** F4
[Cr]own Gn *COVN* CV6 .... **25** G1
[Cr]w Thorns *RUGBYN/HIL* CV21 ... **52** A3

Croxhall St *BDWTH* CV12 .... **6** C2 ▣
Croydon Cl *COVS* CV3 .... **43** G3
Crummock Cl *COVN* CV6 .... **15** F5 ▣
Cryfield Grange Rd
  TLHL/CAN CV4 .... **57** G2
Cryfield Hts *TLHL/CAN* CV4 .... **57** H2
Cubbington Rd *COVN* CV6 .... **16** A5
Cuckoo La *COV* CV1 .... **2** E3 ▣
Culworth Cl *RRUGBY* CV23 .... **52** C2
Culworth Rw *COVN* CV6 .... **25** F2
Cumbria Cl *COVW* CV5 .... **34** C3 ▣
Cunningham Wy North
  RUGBYS/DCH CV22 .... **66** C2 ▣
  RUGBYS/DCH CV22 .... **66** C3 ▣
Curie Cl *RUGBYN/HIL* CV21 .... **68** B1
Curriers Cl *TLHL/CAN* CV4 .... **40** B2
Curtis Rd *COVE* CV2 .... **26** D5
Curzon Av *COVN* CV6 .... **25** G3
Cymbeline Wy
  RUGBYS/DCH CV22 .... **75** H1
Cypress Cft *COVS* CV3 .... **45** F1

D

Daffern Rd *RCOVN/BALC/EX* CV7 .... **6** A4
Daimler Rd *COVN* CV6 .... **35** E1
Daintree Cft *COVS* CV3 .... **43** E2
Dalby Cl *COVS* CV3 .... **45** E2
Dalehouse La *KNWTH* CV8 .... **73** G1
Dale Meadow Cl
  RCOVN/BALC/EX CV7 .... **38** B3
Dale St *RUGBYN/HIL* CV21 .... **51** G5
Daleway Rd *COVS* CV3 .... **58** D1
Dalkeith Av *RUGBYS/DCH* CV22... **66** D5
Dallington Rd *COVN* CV6 .... **24** A5
Dalmeny Rd *TLHL/CAN* CV4 .... **40** B2
Dalton Cl *RRUGBY* CV23 .... **48** D3
Dalton Gdns *COVE* CV2 .... **37** F2
Dalton Rd *BDWTH* CV12 .... **5** H3
  COVW CV5 .... **42** D1
Dame Agnes Gv *COVN* CV6.......... **26** B3
Dane Rd *COVE* CV2 .... **36** B2
Daneswood Rd *COVS* CV3 .... **46** C2 ▣
Daphne Cl *COVE* CV2 .... **16** C5 ▣
Dark La *BDWTH* CV12 .... **5** F4
  COV CV1 .... **35** E2
Darnford Cl *COVE* CV2 .... **27** F4 ▣
Darrach Cl *COVE* CV2 .... **27** E1
Dartmouth Rd *COVE* CV2 .... **36** C1
Darwin Cl *COVE* CV2 .... **27** G5 ▣
Datchet Cl *COVW* CV5 .... **33** G2
D'aubeny Rd *TLHL/CAN* CV4 .... **41** F1
Davenport Rd *COVW* CV5 .... **42** D1
Daventry Rd *COVS* CV3 .... **43** F2
  RUGBYS/DCH CV22 .... **75** H4
David Rd *COV* CV1 .... **3** H5
  RCOVN/BALC/EX CV7 .... **15** H1
  RUGBYS/DCH CV22 .... **66** D4
Davies Rd *RCOVN/BALC/EX* CV7 ... **15** H1
Dawes Cl *COVE* CV2 .... **36** A2
Dawlish Dr *COVS* CV3 .... **43** F4
Dawson Rd *COVS* CV3 .... **36** A5
Days Cl *COV* CV1 .... **3** H2
Day's La *COV* CV1 .... **3** H2
Daytona Dr *COVW* CV5 .... **21** H3
Deacon Cl *RUGBYS/DCH* CV22 .... **68** A3
Deane Pde *RUGBYN/HIL* CV21 .... **69** E4 ▣
Deane Rd *RUGBYN/HIL* CV21 ...... **69** E4
Deanston Cft *COVE* CV2 .... **27** F2
Dean St *COVE* CV2 .... **36** A3
Deans Wy *RCOVN/BALC/EX* CV7 ... **15** F2
De-compton Cl
  RCOVN/BALC/EX CV7 .... **14** C1
Deedmore Rd *COVE* CV2 .... **26** C3
Deegan Cl *COVE* CV2 .... **26** A5
Deepmore Rd
  RUGBYS/DCH CV22 .... **66** D4
Deerdale Wy *COVS* CV3 .... **45** F1
Deerhurst Rd *COVN* CV6 .... **24** D1
Deerings Rd *RUGBYN/HIL* CV21... **69** E4
The Deer Leap *KNWTH* CV8 ..... **73** F1 ▣
Delage Cl *COVE* CV2 .... **16** B4
Delamere Rd *BDWTH* CV12 .... **5** H3
Delaware Rd *COVS* CV3 .... **43** E4
Delhi Av *COVN* CV6 .... **25** E2
Delius St *TLHL/CAN* CV4 .... **32** C3
Dell Cl *COVS* CV3........................... **44** B4
De Montfort Rd *KNWTH* CV8 .... **72** C1
De Montfort Wy *TLHL/CAN* CV4 ... **41** C3
Dempster Rd *BDWTH* CV12 .... **6** A1
Denbigh Rd *COVN* CV6 .... **24** A5
Dencer Dr *KNWTH* CV8 .... **73** H3
Denewood Wy *KNWTH* CV8 ...... **73** G2 ▣
Dengate Dr *RCOVN/BALC/EX* CV7... **38** B2
Denham Av *COVW* CV5 .... **33** F2
Dennis Rd *COVE* CV2 .... **36** B1

Denshaw Cft *COVE* CV2 .... **27** G3
Denton Cl *KNWTH* CV8 .... **72** B1
Dering Cl *COVE* CV2 .... **26** D3
Deronda Cl *BDWTH* CV12 .... **6** A2
Derry Cl *KNWTH* CV8 .... **63** E1 ▣
Dersingham Dr *COVN* CV6 .... **26** B1
Derwent Cl *COVW* CV5 .... **32** C2
  RUGBYN/HIL CV21 .... **52** A3
Derwent Rd *BDWTH* CV12 .... **6** A3
  COVN CV6................................ **24** C1
Despard Rd *COVW* CV5 .... **32** B1
Devereux Cl *TLHL/CAN* CV4 ..... **32** A5 ▣
Devon Gv *COVE* CV2 .... **36** B1
Devoran Cl *RCOVN/BALC/EX* CV7 ... **6** B5
Dewar Gv *RUGBYN/HIL* CV21 ...... **68** C2
Dew Cl *RUGBYS/DCH* CV22 .... **75** H1
Dewsbury Av *COVS* CV3 .... **42** D4
Dial House La *COVW* CV5 .... **32** D2
Diana Dr *COVE* CV2 .... **27** E2
Dickens Rd *COVN* CV6 .... **24** C3
Dickinson Ct *RUGBYS/DCH* CV22.. **67** G3
Diddington La *HIA/OLT* B92 .... **19** E3
Didsbury Rd
  RCOVN/BALC/EX CV7 .... **6** A4 ▣
Digbey Cl *COVW* CV5 .... **23** F5
Dilcock Wy *TLHL/CAN* CV4 .... **40** D2
Dillam Cl *COVN* CV6 .... **16** A4
Dillotford Av *COVS* CV3 .... **43** G3 ▣
Dingle Cl *COVN* CV6 .... **24** C5
Dingley Rd *BDWTH* CV12 .... **7** H3
Discovery Wy *COVS* CV3............... **45** H1
Ditton Cl *RUGBYS/DCH* CV22 ...... **66** C3
Dockers Cl
  RCOVN/BALC/EX CV7 .... **38** C2 ▣
Dodgson Cl *COVN* CV6 .... **16** A4 ▣
Doe Bank La *COV* CV1 .... **34** C3 ▣
Dogberry Cl *COVS* CV3 .... **44** C3
Dolomite Av *COVW* CV5 .... **33** H5
Doncaster Cl *COVE* CV2 .... **26** D4
Done Cerce Cl
  RUGBYS/DCH CV22 .... **75** G4 ▣
Donegal Cl *TLHL/CAN* CV4 .... **41** E2
Donnington Av *COVN* CV6 .... **34** A1
Doone Cl *COVE* CV2 .... **27** E5
Dorchester Wy *COVE* CV2 .... **37** F1
Dormer Harris Av *TLHL/CAN* CV4 .. **32** D5
Dorney Cl *COVW* CV5 .... **42** A1
Dorothy Powell Wy *COVE* CV2 ... **27** F2 ▣
Dorset Rd *COV* CV1 .... **35** E1
Douglas Rd *RUGBYN/HIL* CV21 ... **52** A3
Doulton Cl *COVE* CV2 .... **27** E2 ▣
Dove Cl *BDWTH* CV12 .... **5** G2
Dovecote Cl *COVN* CV6 .... **33** H1
Dovedale *RUGBYN/HIL* CV21 .... **52** A2 ▣
Dovedale Av *COVN* CV6 .... **25** H1
Dover St *COV* CV1 .... **2** B3 ▣
Dowley Cft *COVS* CV3 .... **37** H5
Downderry Wy *COVN* CV6 .... **26** A5
Downing Crs *BDWTH* CV12 .... **6** C1
Downton Cl *COVE* CV2 .... **27** G3 ▣
Dowty Av *BDWTH* CV12 .... **5** F4
Doyle Dr *COVN* CV6 .... **15** H5
Drake St *COVN* CV6 .... **25** F4
Draper Cl *KNWTH* CV8 .... **73** G3
Draper's Flds *COV* CV1 .... **2** D1
  COV CV1 .... **35** E2
Draycott Rd *COVE* CV2 .... **26** B4
Drayton Crs *COVW* CV5................. **32** B1
Drayton Leys *RUGBYS/DCH* CV22.. **67** G5
Drayton Rd *BDWTH* CV12............. **6** C3
Drew Crs *KNWTH* CV8 .... **73** E3
Dreyer Cl *RUGBYS/DCH* CV22 ..... **66** C2
The Drive *COVE* CV2 .... **36** D3
Dronfield Rd *COVE* CV2 .... **36** B3
Droylsdon Park Rd *COVS* CV3 ..... **58** D1
Druid Rd *COVE* CV2 .... **36** D3
Drummond Cl *COVN* CV6 .... **24** B4 ▣
Drury La *RUGBYN/HIL* CV21 .... **67** G1 ▣
Drybrooks Cl
  RCOVN/BALC/EX CV7 .... **38** B3 ▣
Dryden Cl *KNWTH* CV8 .... **72** D4
Dryden Pl *RUGBYS/DCH* CV22 ..... **67** E1 ▣
Dryden Wk *RUGBYS/DCH* CV22 ... **67** E1 ▣
Dudley Rd *KNWTH* CV8 .... **72** D5
Dudley St *COVN* CV6 ....▪.......... **26** A2
Duffy Pl *RUGBYN/HIL* CV21 .... **69** E4
Dugdale Rd *COVN* CV6 .... **24** C5
Duggins La *RCOVN/BALC/EX* CV7 .. **39** H1
Duke Barn Fld *COVE* CV2 .... **36** A1
Duke St *COVW* CV5 .... **34** B4
  RUGBYN/HIL CV21 .... **51** G5 ▣
Dulverton Av *COVW* CV5 .... **33** H2
Duncan Dr *RUGBYS/DCH* CV22 ... **75** H1
Dunchurch Cl
  RCOVN/BALC/EX CV7 .... **38** B2 ▣
Dunchurch Hwy *COVW* CV5......... **23** G5
  COVW CV5 .... **33** G3
  TLHL/CAN CV4 .... **33** G4

Dunchurch Rd
  RUGBYS/DCH CV22 .... **67** G3
Duncroft Av *COVN* CV6 .... **24** B4
Dunhill Av *TLHL/CAN* CV4 .... **32** C3
Dunnerdale *RUGBYN/HIL* CV21 ... **52** B3
Dunnose Cl *COVN* CV6 .... **25** G3 ▣
Dunrose Cl *COVE* CV2 .... **37** E4
Dunsmore Av *COVS* CV3 .... **44** C4 ▣
  RUGBYS/DCH CV22 .... **68** C4
Dunsmore Heath
  RUGBYS/DCH CV22 .... **75** G4 ▣
Dunster Pl *COVN* CV6 .... **15** F5
Dunsville Dr *COVE* CV2 .... **27** F3
Dunvegan Cl *COVS* CV3 .... **37** G4
  KNWTH CV8 .... **73** G3
Durbar Av *COVN* CV6..................... **25** F3
Durham Cl *RCOVN/BALC/EX* CV7... **14** B4
Durham Crs *COVW* CV5 .... **23** F4
Dutton Rd *COVE* CV2 .... **16** D5
Dyer's La *KNWTH* CV8 .... **63** E1
Dymond Rd *COVN* CV6 .... **15** E5
Dysart Cl *COV* CV1 .... **3** G1
Dyson Cl *RUGBYN/HIL* CV21 .... **68** D3
Dyson St *TLHL/CAN* CV4 .... **32** C3

E

Eacott Cl *COVN* CV6 .... **14** C5 ▣
Eagle St *COV* CV1 .... **35** F1 ▣
Eagle St East *COV* CV1 .... **35** F1
The Earl's Cft *COVS* CV3 .... **43** F2
Earlsdon Av North *COVW* CV5 ..... **34** B5
Earlsdon Av South *COVW* CV5 ..... **42** C1
Earlsdon St *COVW* CV5 .... **42** B1
Earl St *BDWTH* CV12 .... **6** C3
  COV CV1 .... **2** E4
  RUGBYN/HIL CV21 .... **67** H1
Easedale Cl *COVS* CV3 .... **42** D3
East Av *BDWTH* CV12 .... **6** D3
  COVE CV2 .... **36** A3
Eastbourne Cl *COVN* CV6 .... **24** A5 ▣
East Car Park Rd *BHAMNEC* B40... **8** B4
Eastcote La *HIA/OLT* B92 .... **28** C1
Eastcotes *TLHL/CAN* CV4 .... **33** F5
Eastern Green Rd *COVW* CV5 ...... **32** D3
Eastfield Pl *RUGBYN/HIL* CV21 .. **67** G1 ▣
Eastlands Gv *COVW* CV5 .... **34** A2
Eastlands Pl
  RUGBYN/HIL CV21 .... **68** B1 ▣
Eastlands Rd *RUGBYN/HIL* CV21... **68** B1
Eastleigh Av *COVW* CV5 .... **42** B2 ▣
East St *COV* CV1 .... **3** H3
  RUGBYN/HIL CV21 .... **52** B5
East Union St *RUGBYS/DCH* CV22.. **67** G2
East Wy *BHAMNEC* B40 .... **8** B5
  HIA/OLT B92 .... **8** C5
Eastwood Gv *RUGBYN/HIL* CV21... **69** G4
Easy La *RUGBYN/HIL* CV21 .... **67** F1 ▣
Eathorpe Cl *COVE* CV2 .... **26** C2 ▣
Eaton Rd *COV* CV1 .... **2** C6
Eaves Green La
  RCOVN/BALC/EX CV7 .... **21** E3
Ebbw Vale Ter *COVS* CV3 .... **43** F2
Ebourne Cl *KNWTH* CV8 .... **73** E3
Ebro Crs *COVS* CV3 .... **37** F5
Eburne Rd *COVE* CV2 .... **16** C5
Eccles Cl *COVE* CV2 .... **26** D5
Ecton Leys *RUGBYS/DCH* CV22 ... **67** G5
Edale Wy *COVN* CV6 .... **26** A4 ▣
Eden Cft *KNWTH* CV8 .... **73** F3
Eden Rd *RCOVN/BALC/EX* CV7 .... **27** G2
  RUGBYN/HIL CV21 .... **68** D3
Eden St *COVN* CV6 .... **25** H4
Edgecote Cl *RUGBYN/HIL* CV21 .. **68** B3
Edgefield Rd *COVE* CV2 .... **27** G3
Edgehill Pl *TLHL/CAN* CV4........... **32** A5
Edgwick Rd *COVN* CV6 .... **25** H4
Edinburgh Wy *RRUGBY* CV23 ..... **50** B4 ▣
Edingale Rd *COVE* CV2 .... **27** F3 ▣
Edmund Rd *COV* CV1 .... **35** F1
Edward Bailey Cl *COVS* CV3......... **45** E2
Edward Rd *BDWTH* CV12 .... **6** C3
  COVN CV6................................ **14** C5
Edwards Gv *KNWTH* CV8 .... **73** G2
Edward St *COVN* CV6 .... **35** G1 ▣
  RUGBYN/HIL CV21 .... **51** F5
Edward Tyler Rd *BDWTH* CV12 .... **6** A4
Edyth Rd *COVE* CV2 .... **37** E2
Egerton Cl *RUGBYN/HIL* CV21 .... **51** F1
Elborow St *RUGBYN/HIL* CV21 .. **67** G1 ▣
Elderberry Wy *COVE* CV2 .... **26** B5 ▣
Elder Cl *RUGBYS/DCH* CV22 .... **66** B4
Eld Rd *COVN* CV6 .... **25** G2
Elgar Rd *COVN* CV6 .... **26** B3
Eliot Ct *RUGBYS/DCH* CV22 .... **67** E1
Elizabeth Wy *KNWTH* CV8 .... **72** C1